The Coming Apocalypse

A Study of Replacement Theology vs. God's Faithfulness in the End-Times

DR. RENALD E. SHOWERS

The Coming Apocalypse

A Study of Replacement Theology
vs. God's Faithfulness in the End-Times

DR. RENALD E. SHOWERS

The Friends of Israel, Inc.
P.O. Box 908 • Bellmawr, NJ 08099

THE COMING APOCALYPSE
A Study of Replacement Theology
vs. God's Faithfulness in the End-Times

Dr. Renald E. Showers

Copyright © 2009 by The Friends of Israel Gospel Ministry, Inc.
P.O. Box 908, Bellmawr, NJ 08099

Sixth Printing 2019

ISBN-10 0 915540 07 X
ISBN-13 978 0 915540 07 5
Library of Congress Catalog Card Number: 2009923216

Cover design by Waveline Direct, LLC., Mechanicsburg, PA

For other great titles by Renald Showers, visit our website at *foi.org*.

Table of Contents

CHAPTER 1

ISRAEL AND REPLACEMENT THEOLOGY

While speaking at a conference many years ago, I related the fact that on November 29, 1947, the UN General Assembly approved dividing the British-ruled land of Palestine into two states: an independent State of Israel in its ancient homeland and an independent Arab state.

After the meeting a group of men who claimed to be Christians confronted me. "The United Nations," they said, "never approved the Jews being given a division of the land of Palestine for an independent State of Israel in the Middle East."

"How can you say that?" I asked. "The history books record the United Nations approval."

They shot back, "It doesn't matter what the history books say. That never happened!"

"You can go to the United Nations headquarters in New York and read the record of that approval," I told them.

Unfazed, they continued: "It doesn't matter if the record is there," one told me. "That never happened. The Jews had no governing authority to go into Palestine and establish a new State of Israel. They went in there totally on their own initiative and drove out the Arab people already there. As a result, the State of Israel has no legitimate right to exist in the Middle East. It should be driven into the Mediterranean Sea."

These men subscribed to what we today call Replacement Theology, a theological view of the world that claims God is forever finished with Israel as a nation. Therefore, God's promise in the

Abrahamic Covenant to give the physical descendants of Abraham, Isaac, and Jacob the land of Canaan as an eternal inheritance is no longer in effect with national Israel.

It is well known that advocates of Islam reject Israel's right to own the land. However, there are also Christians who do so, contrary to the Bible. They claim that because the majority of Israel failed to embrace Jesus Christ during His First Coming, God forever rejected Israel as a nation. They believe God repealed or terminated the Abrahamic Covenant, that Israel has forfeited ownership of the land, and that the Covenant's everlasting nature was abrogated.

According to this view, God will save individual Jewish people, but He has no present or future program for Israel as a nation. He has rejected Israel as His people and replaced Israel with the church. The technical name for this view is Supersessionism. But it is more commonly known as Replacement Theology. And it is wrong.

The Beginning and Early History of Replacement Theology

The church began in the early 30s A.D. It was centered first in Jerusalem and for several years was overwhelmingly Jewish in membership. Many of these early Jewish Christians seemed to have no intention of separating from Judaism.[1] They believed their faith was the fulfillment, not the enemy, of the faith of their fathers.[2] Thus they optimistically thought the majority of their fellow Jews would adopt their belief that Jesus of Nazareth was the Messiah.

But the majority rejected that belief.[3] Sadly, unbelieving Jewish people began to persecute the early Christians severely.[4] Thus the earliest persecution of the church consisted of Jewish people persecuting other Jewish people for religious reasons. This situation forced many of the early Christians to scatter from Jerusalem to other areas where they preached the gospel to other groups. As a result, Samaritans and Gentiles began to be reached with the

8

gospel and to come into the church.[5] Before the end of the first century of the church's existence, it "had become predominantly non-Jewish in its membership."[6] As a result, Jewish persecution of the church declined greatly.[7]

The rejection of Jesus as the Messiah by the majority of Jews of that time "had consequences of major importance for both Christianity and Judaism."[8] As Christianity became predominantly Gentile in membership, it began to change significantly in contrast to what it was when mainly Jewish.[9] Within one hundred years after the apostles of Jesus Christ were gone, the "majority of Gentile Christians regarded the Jewish Scriptures as authoritative" but began to think "of themselves as the true spiritual heirs of Israel" and "claimed for themselves the promises which the Hebrews held that Yahweh had made to them."[10]

According to Adolph Harnack, "The Christians held that, the Jews having been rejected by God, they themselves had become the chosen people."[11] In other words, they claimed that God permanently ended Israel's unique relationship with Him as a nation and replaced it with the church as His unique people. Thus the Christians were now the Israel of God.

Some anti-Semitic, Gentile church leaders played a key role in this significant shift away from the original understanding of the Scriptures regarding Israel's relationship with God. Some resorted to new methods of biblical interpretation and wrote rebuttals with varying degrees of anti-Semitic content.

JUSTIN MARTYR (A.D. 100–165), a Christian apologist who defended Christianity against its enemies, made the following claim in his work *Dialogue of Justin Martyr With Trypho a Jew:* Christians "are the true Israelitic race."[12] He also asserted that the biblical expression *the seed of Jacob,* when properly understood, now referred to Christians, not Jews.[13] This was a significant shift in the understanding of Scripture.

TERTULLIAN (A.D. 160–220), a prominent church theologian from North Africa, wrote an anti-Semitic discourse titled *An Answer to the Jews* around A.D. 200. He interpreted God's statements to Rebekah concerning the twins (Esau and Jacob) in her womb (Gen. 25:23) in the following manner: Esau, the older brother, represents the Jewish people; Jacob, the younger brother, represents the Christians. He indicated that God thereby revealed that the Christians would overcome the Jews, and the Jewish people would serve the Christians.[14]

ORIGEN (A.D. 185–254), president of the influential school of theology in Alexandria, Egypt, greatly influenced the church's acceptance of the allegorical, or spiritualizing, method of interpreting the Bible. This method contrasts sharply with the literal-historical-grammatical method. The allegorical method permitted Origen to read almost any meaning he desired into the language of the Bible. It allowed him to claim that the word *Israel* in the Bible can mean the church, not national Israel. It also led him into heresy in certain areas of doctrine. For example, he rejected the concept of physical resurrection and believed in universal salvation for all human beings and fallen angels.[15]

Concerning Origen's approach to biblical interpretation, church historian Philip Schaff wrote, "His great defect is the neglect of the grammatical and historical sense and his constant desire to find a hidden mystic meaning. . . . His allegorical interpretation is ingenious, but often runs far away from the text and degenerates into the merest caprice."[16]

DIONYSIUS (A.D. 190–264), influential bishop of Alexandria, succeeded in "asserting the allegorical interpretation of the prophets as the only legitimate exegesis."[17]

CYPRIAN (A.D. 195–258), bishop of Carthage, wrote *Three Books of Testimonies Against the Jews*. He stated that in this work, he "endeavoured to show that the Jews, according to what had before been foretold, had departed from God, and had lost God's favour, which had been given them in past time, and had been promised them for the future; while the Christians had succeeded to their place, deserving well of the Lord by faith, and coming out of all nations and from the whole world."[18]

Like Tertullian, he interpreted God's statements to Rebekah

concerning the twins in her womb (Gen. 25:23) in the following allegorical manner: Esau, the older brother, represents the Jews; Jacob, the younger brother, represents the Christians.[19] The implication: The Christians have inherited the birthright that the Jewish people forfeited. He also declared, "The Gentiles rather than the Jews attain to the kingdom of heaven."[20]

JOHN CHRYSOSTOM (A.D. 347–407), the greatest preacher in the history of the Eastern church, delivered messages *Against the Jews* in Antioch of Syria.[21] According to *The Jewish Encyclopedia*, Chrysostom; Cyril (376–444), bishop of Alexandria; and Ambrose (340–397), bishop of Milan, "potently affected the fate of the Jewish people."[22]

These examples demonstrate how Replacement Theology developed quite early in the history of the church.

The Effects of Replacement Theology on the Church

Over the next several centuries, Replacement Theology played a significant role in producing major changes in two areas of organized Christendom: ecclesiology and eschatology.[23]

Effects on Ecclesiology. In the area of ecclesiology (the nature and function of the church) Replacement Theology contributed significantly to the development of Roman Catholicism. As a result of Gentile leaders concluding that the church was now the Israel of God, Gentiles began to appropriate to the church things that God had instituted specifically for the nation of Israel.

The book of Acts indicates that the original church leaders were elders. But since God gave Israel priests as mediators between Himself and the people of Israel, early Gentile church leaders began to call church leaders priests.

Since God gave Israel a multitiered priesthood with one high priest at the top, regular priests under him, and Levites under them to serve in Israel's Tabernacle and Temple, Replacement Theology church leaders progressively built a multitiered priesthood for the church. It consisted of bishops, monarchal bishops, metropolitan bishops, archbishops, cardinals, and one high priest: the pope.

Since God gave Israel continuing blood sacrifices with animals, Replacement Theology church leaders progressively changed the significance of the church's communion service from a memorial of Christ's death for the sins of mankind ("do this in remembrance of Me," Lk. 22:19) to a continuing sacrifice for sins. This new view claimed that in communion, the bread is transformed into Christ's flesh, and the wine is transformed into Christ's blood. Thus every time communion is observed, Christ is sacrificed again for sin. Because this view asserts that in communion one substance is transformed into another, it became known as transubstantiation.[24]

This continuing-sacrifice view of communion is contrary to Christ's cry from the cross, "It is finished!" (Jn. 19:30). Christ indicated that His sacrificial death for mankind's sins was finished when He died on the cross. If He has to be continually sacrificed for sins, then His death for the sins of mankind was incomplete. But because it was finished, the apostle Paul wrote, "For the death that He died, He died to sin once for all" (Rom. 6:10).

In addition, the writer of the book of Hebrews stated that Jesus "does not need daily," as do Israel's "high priests, to offer up sacrifices, first for His own sins and then for the people's, for this He did once for all when He offered up Himself" (Heb. 7:27). He also stated, "Christ was offered once to bear the sins of many" (9:28). The apostle Peter asserted the same when he stated that Christ "Himself bore our sins in His own body on the tree" (while on the cross, 1 Pet. 2:24) and that "Christ also suffered once for sins, the just for the unjust, that He might bring us to God, being put to death in the flesh" (3:18).

Effects on Eschatology. In the area of eschatology, early Replacement Theology prompted the rejection of the church's original view called Chiliasm (from the Greek word for "one thousand"). Chiliasm taught that Jesus Christ will return to the earth in a Second Coming, establish God's theocracy as an earthly political Kingdom of God, and administer God's rule for the final thousand years of this present earth's history. Today this view is called Premillennialism. Chiliasm was the predominant view of orthodox Christianity from the first to the third centuries A.D.

Before the church began, ancient Jews—on the basis of Old Testament prophecies—believed and taught that in the future, God's Messiah would establish God's theocracy as an earthly, political Kingdom of God and that, as God's earthly representative, He would administer God's rule over the entire world for the last age of this present earth's history.

However, despite the fact that this view of eschatology was based on Old Testament prophecies, was taught by Christ and His apostles, and was the church's original view, the Replacement Theology of some anti-Semitic, Gentile church leaders prompted them to reject Chiliasm because they considered it a Jewish view.

As early as A.D. 170, some leaders of the Greek church in the East began to reject Chiliasm. There was a strong anti-Semitic spirit in the Eastern church. Because many Jewish people of Jesus' day rejected Him and many of their successors refused to believe in Him, Gentiles who professed to be Christians increasingly called Jewish people "Christ-killers" and developed a strong bias against anything Jewish. And because Chiliasm embodied the same eschatological hope that had motivated the Jewish people for centuries, that view became increasingly "stigmatized as 'Jewish' and consequently 'heretical'" by Eastern Gentile Christians.[25]

Some rejected the prophetic Scriptures from which Chiliasm was derived. For example, Dionysius believed that the rejection of "'Jewish' chiliasm would never be secure so long as the Apocalypse of John passed for an apostolic writing and kept its place" in the Bible.[26] He so prejudiced the Greek church against the canonicity of that biblical book that the church removed it from its canon of Scripture during the fourth century and kept it out for several centuries; "and consequently chiliasm remained in its grave."[27]

The Western, or Latin, church held to Chiliasm longer than the Greek church in the East. In the West, Chiliasm "was still a point of 'orthodoxy' in the 4th century."[28] But after the fourth century the Western church began to join the revolt against Chiliasm. Teaching from the Greek church was brought to the West by such influential church leaders as Jerome and Ambrose. As a result of being taught by Greek theologians in the East for several years, Jerome (A.D. 345–420) declared that he had been delivered from "Jewish opinions"; and he ridiculed the early beliefs of Chiliasm.[29]

AMBROSE (A.D. 340–397), influential bishop of Milan, used the Jewish people as "a type of the infidel."[30] He regarded the Jewish soul to be "irrevocably perverse and incapable of any good thought" and asserted that "burning a Jewish synagogue was not a crime."[31] Ambrose was the spiritual mentor of Augustine.

AUGUSTINE (A.D. 354–430) became the bishop of Hippo and influenced the future direction of organized Christendom more than any person since the apostle Paul. Augustine's *Tract Against the Jews* was so influential a publication that derogatory arguments against Jewish people throughout the Middle Ages were usually called "Augustinian."[32]

In the early years of his Christian faith, Augustine held the Chiliasm view of the early church. However, it appears that Ambrose's and Jerome's anti-Semitic views motivated him to reject Chiliasm because of the thought that it was "Jewish." Another factor that certainly prompted Augustine's rejection of Chiliasm was the Greek philosophy that influenced his thinking.

Before Augustine became a Christian, he was deeply immersed in the study of philosophy, much of which asserted the inherent evil of the physical and material and the inherent goodness of the totally spiritual. That philosophy continued to leave its mark on him after his conversion. It prompted him to regard the Chiliasm view of an earthly, political Kingdom of God with great physical and material blessings as being carnal. To his way of thinking, in order for the Kingdom of God to be good, it had to be spiritual in nature. Thus, "for him the millennium had become a spiritual state into which the Church collectively had entered at Pentecost . . . and which the individual Christian might already enjoy through mystical communion with God."[33]

In order to avoid the implications of some of the millennial passages in the Bible, Augustine applied the allegorical method of interpretation to the prophets and The Revelation of Jesus Christ. For example, he interpreted the first resurrection referred to by the apostle John in conjunction with the establishment of Christ's millennial reign (Rev. 20:4–6) not as the future, bodily resurrection of believers but as the present, spiritual resurrection of the soul, which takes place at the new birth.[34]

In place of the Chiliasm view that he rejected, Augustine developed a new eschatological view called Amillennialism. *Amillennialism* means "no Millennium." Thus this view denies a future, earthly political Kingdom of God over which Christ will administer God's rule for the last thousand years of this present earth's history. In this view, Augustine developed the idea that the church is the Kingdom of God foretold in such Scriptures as Daniel 2 and 7 and Revelation 20.

In his book *The City of God*, Augustine became the first person to teach that the organized catholic (universal) church is the Messianic Kingdom and that the Millennium began with the First Coming of Christ.[35] Augustine wrote, "The saints reign with Christ during the same thousand years, understood in the same way, that is, of the time of His first coming,"[36] and, "Therefore the Church even now is the kingdom of Christ, and the kingdom of heaven. Accordingly, even now His saints reign with Him."[37] According to this view, the history of this present earth will end at Christ's Second Coming; and the future, eternal state will begin.

"Augustine's allegorical millennialism became the official doctrine of the church," and Chiliasm went underground.[38] Some aspects of Chiliasm were even branded as heretical.[39]

Thus Replacement Theology, together with other factors, played a key role in both the rejection of the original eschatological view of the church and the development of a new view: Amillennialism.[40]

Throughout the Middle Ages, the Roman Catholic Church adopted, maintained, and strongly advocated Replacement Theology and Augustine's amillennial view. Believing itself to be the Kingdom of God on Earth foretold in the Bible, it believed it had the right to enforce its beliefs and policies on all people, including political rulers, pagans, and Jews. As a result, it developed into a powerful religious-political machine that dominated every aspect of life in Western Europe—even to the point of setting up, dominating, removing, and humiliating kings and emperors. This power played a key role in the Roman Catholic Church's persecution of Jews for centuries to come.

The reformers of the 16th-century Protestant Reformation broke away from the Roman Catholic Church in several critical areas of ecclesiology and doctrine. Contrary to Roman Catholic teaching, the reformers emphasized the following New Testament truths: (1) Justification by faith alone, not faith plus works. (2) The priesthood of every believer. God intends every believer to have a ministry; He did not intend the church to have a multitiered priesthood that does the work of ministry apart from the laypeople. (3) The Bible—not a man, such as the pope, or an organization, such as the church—is to be the authority for faith and practice.

But in the area of eschatology, the Lutheran, Reformed, and Anglican reformers rejected Chiliasm (today known as Premillennialism) as being "Jewish opinions."[41] They maintained the amillennial view that the Roman Catholic Church adopted from Augustine.[42] As a result, in much the same manner as the Roman Catholic Church, they believed they had the right to enforce their beliefs and policies on everyone, including the Jewish people.

Their view of Chiliasm as "Jewish opinions" seems to indicate that Replacement Theology, with its anti-Semitic tendencies, played a key role in their rejection of the church's original eschatological view and their acceptance of Amillennialism. Nevertheless, not all the reformers advocated persecuting the Jews. However, one certainly did.

MARTIN LUTHER. Martin Luther, who began the Reformation in Germany in 1517, adopted a strong anti-Semitic disposition toward the Jewish people. *The Jewish Encyclopedia* states that during his early years as a reformer, Luther was "full of compassion for their misery and enthusiastic for their conversion to Christianity," but "toward the end of his life, he denounces them in unmeasured terms, saying that it is useless to convert any Jew, and accusing them of a relentless hatred of Christianity and of all the crimes which their enemies ever charged them with—well-poisoning, ritual murder, cowardly assassinations of their patients, etc. He wishes the princes to persecute them mercilessly and the preachers to set the mob against them."[43]

"He repeatedly urges that their synagogues be burned, and is sorry that he can not destroy them with hell-fire. He further advises that their houses be torn down, their books taken from them, their rabbis prohibited from teaching; that no safe-conduct be granted them; that their usury be prohibited; that their public worship be interdicted; that they be forced to do the hardest labor; and he admonishes everybody to deal with them in a merciless manner, 'even as Moses did, who slew three thousand of them in the wilderness.'"

He admonished "his readers not to have the slightest intercourse with the Jews" and said, "If I had power over them I would assemble their most prominent men and demand that they prove that we Christians do not worship the one God, under the penalty of having their tongues torn out through the back of their necks."[44] Luther argued that "the sufferings of the Jews are the just punishment for their rejection of Jesus."[45] Adolf Hitler read Luther's statements to the Germans to justify the systematic elimination of millions of Jewish people in the Holocaust of World War II.

COVENANT THEOLOGY. Covenant Theology began to develop as a system of theology in the Reformed churches of Switzerland and Germany in the 16th and 17th centuries. It passed to the Netherlands, Scotland, and England[46] and was introduced to America primarily through the Puritans. Advocates of Covenant

Theology adopted Replacement Theology in relationship to the nation of Israel. As a result, they claimed that, because Israel on the whole rejected Christ as its Messiah, God forever rejected the nation of Israel as His people and replaced Israel with the church. Thus the church was now the Israel of God and inheritor of the blessings He promised to national Israel. This view meant, then, that national Israel lost forever its rightful claim of ownership of the land that God gave to it in ancient times. If carried to its logical conclusion, it also meant that the church, including Gentiles, is the rightful owner of the land.

Advocates of Covenant Theology continue to hold that view today. This does not mean they necessarily hate Jewish people and believe they should be persecuted. But it does mean that their adoption of Replacement Theology has affected their view of Israel's ownership of the land and its right to exist as a nation in the Middle East.

In order to adopt Replacement Theology, people must mix two different systems of biblical interpretation. They employ the allegorical method when interpreting passages that deal with national Israel and future prophecy but use the historical-grammatical method for other portions of the Bible.

This double method of interpreting the Bible seems strange in light of two facts. First, Covenant Theology recognizes that the historical-grammatical method of interpreting the Bible is normal. That method focuses on historical background and grammar to determine the correct meaning of a passage. Words are given the common, ordinary meaning they had in the culture and time in which the passage was written. Covenant Theology also recognizes that employing another method of interpretation could lead to disaster when seeking the meaning of a passage. It could lead the interpreter away from the meaning the passage was intended to convey when it was written.

The allegorical method is a different method of interpretation that is opposite to the historical-grammatical method. It does not give words the common, ordinary meaning they had in the culture and time in which the passage was written. Instead, words are assigned different meanings. Thus, according to this method, the word *Israel* does not have to mean the nation of Israel. It could mean the church. In addition, according to this method, prophetic promises of future blessing for Israel do not have to be fulfilled with the nation of Israel. Instead, they are to be fulfilled with the church. This method gives the interpreter, not the author, the authority to determine the meaning a passage was intended to convey.

Second, a major problem with the allegorical method of interpreting unfulfilled, prophetic passages of the Bible is that, thus far, the prophetic Scriptures that have been fulfilled have been fulfilled in accordance with the historical-grammatical method, not the allegorical method. This important fact would seem to indicate the manner in which God intends all prophetic passages to be interpreted. So by what authority does a person assume the right to interpret them allegorically?

The Effects of Replacement Theology on the Jewish People

A sample survey of history demonstrates that Replacement Theology has had a devastating effect on the Jewish people.

When Constantine, the first Roman emperor to declare himself a Christian, became sole ruler of the entire empire in A.D. 323, he began an increasingly "hostile policy toward the Jews."[47] In 329 "the death penalty was ordained for those who embraced the Jewish faith, as well as for Jews versed in the Law who aided them. . . . An edict was issued forbidding marriages between Jews and Christians, and imposing the death penalty upon any Jew who should transgress this law."[48] Several of these laws referred to Judaism as "an ignominious" or "bestial sect."[49] During Constantine's reign, "Sylvester, Bishop of Rome, Paul, afterwards Bishop of Constantinople, the new capital, and Eusebius of Caesarea, the first historian of the Church, did not fail to incite the inhabitants of the empire against the Jews."[50]

Theodosius I, Roman emperor from 379 to 395, who decreed that Christianity was to be the only religion allowed in the empire, declared that "marriage between a Jew and a Christian must be legally regarded as adultery."[51]

Theodosius II, Roman emperor from 408 to 450, "prohibited the Jews from building new synagogues."[52] During his reign, Cyril, bishop of Alexandria, was allowed to abuse "the Jews and to drive them out of that town. He assembled the Christian mob, incited them against the Jews by his excessive fanaticism, forced his way into the synagogues, of which he took possession for the Christians," and handed over the Jews' property "to be pillaged by the mob, ever greedy of plunder."[53]

Justinian I, emperor of the eastern Roman Empire from 527 to 565 and a professing Christian, passed a law requiring Jewish people to occupy the most disliked civil offices in government. He forbade them to observe Passover before the Christians' Easter, dictated what could and could not be done in synagogue services, and levied heavy taxes on them.[54] He also ordered synagogues to be turned into churches and forbade Jews to own Christian slaves.[55]

In 589 King Reccared of Spain united with a Roman Catholic synod to prohibit the Jewish people "from contracting marriages with the Christians, from acquiring Christian slaves, and from holding public offices," and requiring that children born of Jewish-Christian "intermarriages were to be forcibly baptized" as Christians.[56]

Around A.D. 629 Dagobert, ruler of the Frankish empire, decreed "that the entire Jewish population of the Frankish empire must either embrace Christianity before a certain day, or be treated as enemies and be put to death."[57]

Near the end of the seventh century a new law was passed requiring that all Jews in Spain "be enslaved and that their sons be taken away from them at the age of seven and be reared as Christians."[58]

In 729 Leo III, emperor of the Eastern Roman Empire (also known as Byzantium), ordered all the Jewish people of that empire "to embrace the Christianity of the Greek Church, under pain of severe punishment." Many reluctantly submitted to baptism, but many migrated to the Crimea.[59]

In ninth-century France, the anti-Semitic Roman Catholic bishops of Lyons—Agobard and Amolo—tried to overthrow the liberties and privileges Emperors Charlemagne and Louis had granted the Jews. They wanted to prevent Jewish people from holding any office or position of honor, such as a judgeship; to prohibit Jewish people from appearing in public during Easter week; to require Jewish people "to pay utmost respect" to the Christian clergy; and to remove children from parents who converted to Judaism.[60]

The first persecution in Germany took place in the 11th century. In 1005 the chaplain to Duke Conrad—a relative of Henry II, emperor of the Holy Roman Empire—converted from Christianity to Judaism. Later the convert wrote an attack on Christianity. This may have stirred up the anger of the Roman Catholic clergy against the Jews in Germany. It definitely aroused the emperor's anger. He appointed one of his clergy to write a reply. In 1012 Henry II ordered the Jewish people expelled from Mainz, and possibly from other Jewish centers, for their refusal to be baptized as Christians.[61]

Pope Gregory VII desired to humble the Jewish people and take from them "the respect and honors which they had acquired by their merit."[62] At the 1078 Roman Catholic Church congress in Rome, he established a church law "to the effect that the Jews should hold no office in Christendom, and exercise no supremacy whatever over the Christians."[63] He intended this law to change the situation in Spain, where King Alfonso had Jewish people in key positions of leadership.

In 1080 Pope Gregory sent Alfonso a letter that included the following statements: "We admonish your Highness that you must cease to suffer the Jews to rule over the Christians and exercise authority over them. For to allow the Christians to be subordinate to the Jews, and to subject them to their judgment, is the same as oppressing God's Church and exalting Satan's synagogue. To wish to please God's enemies means to treat Christ himself with contumely [contempt]."[64]

The Crusades of the Middle Ages were Western European military excursions to Eastern Europe and the Middle East for the primary purpose of liberating the Holy Land from Muslim rule and helping the Byzantine Empire prevent the Muslim conquest of Eastern Europe. But they were disastrous for the Jews. In the first three Crusades (A.D. 1096, 1145–47, and 1189–90), unruly mobs who accompanied the soldiers killed thousands of Jewish people, looted their possessions, and destroyed their homes in Germany, France, England, and other areas.[65] "They prepared the way for the anti-Jewish legislation of Innocent III, and formed the turning point in the medieval history of the Jews."[66]

Innocent III, pope from 1198 to 1216, was the most powerful pope in the history of the Roman Catholic Church. He presided over the Fourth Lateran Council in 1215. According to eminent historian Dr. Heinrich Graetz, this pope "was an embittered enemy of the Jews and Judaism, and dealt severer blows against them than any of his predecessors."[67] His attitude was as follows: "The Jews, like the fratricide Cain, are doomed to wander about the earth as fugitives and vagabonds, and their faces must be covered with shame. They are under no circumstances to be protected by Christian princes, but, on the contrary, to be condemned to serfdom."[68] He threatened to excommunicate any political rulers who would not oppress the Jewish people.[69] Innocent III and the Fourth Lateran Council decreed that Jews age 12 and older in all Christian countries must wear at all times a distinguishing badge of color that identified them publicly as Jews.[70]

King Philip Augustus of France became "one of the greatest Jew-hating kings in history."[71] Although he did not believe the horrendous lie being circulated in Europe that the Jewish people killed Christian children at Passover and drank their blood, he nevertheless acted toward them as if it were true.[72] In 1180 he had all Jewish people living on his personal land arrested while praying in their synagogues and imprisoned. He made wealthy Jews paupers and had all the Jewish people expelled from his province in 1181. They lost all their possessions except what they could carry with them. He allowed their deserted synagogues to be used as churches.[73] The only way these Jewish people could retain ownership of their properties was to be baptized as Christians.[74] In the end, he was responsible for the deaths of many.[75]

During the reign of King Edward I of England, Jews were forbidden to take interest from the loan of money. Because of a false rumor that they had circulated counterfeit money, all the Jews of England—including wives and children—were imprisoned in 1278, some temporarily and some for life; others were expelled from the country and their property taken. Because of another false rumor that some Jewish people had crucified a Christian child, many Jews in London were torn apart by horses in 1279. Any Jewish people who showed disrespect to Christian emblems were to be executed.

In 1280 the Jewish people were required to listen to Christian preaching. A famous Franciscan monk, Duns Scotus, told the king that it was his duty to take Jewish children from their parents, teach them Christian beliefs, and use any means necessary to force the parents to receive Christian baptism. In 1290 Edward I expelled all the Jews from England and executed any who did not leave. Those expelled went to France but shortly were banished from there as well.[76]

A horrendous holocaust against the Jewish people took place in Germany and Austria in 1298. Because of a report that Jews in the town of Rottingen, Franconia, had desecrated the sacred Roman Catholic host, nobleman Rindfleisch of that town led a mob to burn the Jews of Rottingen at the stake. He and the mob went to other towns in Franconia and Bavaria, killing all Jews except those who converted to Christianity. The execution of Jewish people spread from Germany to Austria. In less than six months approximately 120 Jewish congregations consisting of 100,000 Jews perished.[77]

Graetz, author of the exhaustive work, *History of the Jews*, wrote:

> *From the thirteenth till the sixteenth century, the persecutions and massacres of the Jews increased with frightful rapidity and in intensity, and only alternated with inhuman decrees issued both by the Church and the state, the aim and purport of all of which were to humiliate the Jews, to brand them with calumny and to drive them to suicide. . . . The nations of Europe emulated one another in exercising their cruelty upon the Jews; and it was always the clergy who, in the name of a religion of love, stirred up this undying hatred. It mattered little to the Jews whether they lived under a strict government or under anarchy, for they suffered under the one no less than under the other.* [78]

In 1336–1337 two German noblemen with 5,000 peasants slaughtered thousands of Jewish people through various forms of torture and execution in Bavaria, Bohemia, Moravia, and Austria.[79]

The Black Death plague, which destroyed a fourth of mankind, came to Europe with devastating force in 1348. A rumor claimed that the Jews instigated the plague by poisoning the wells and rivers of Europe in order to eliminate all the Christians. As the rumor spread and false confessions of guilt were forced from suspects through torture, mob violence against the Jewish people began to break out and spread across the European countryside. Thousands of innocent Jews were put to death in France, Spain, Switzerland, Germany, Austria, Poland, and Belgium, primarily by burning at the stake.[80]

For quite a few years Jewish people had enjoyed freedom, privileges, and prosperity in Spain. But that suddenly changed in March 1391. As a result of the hateful preaching of Ferdinand Martinez, a Roman Catholic priest, mob violence broke out against the Jews in the city of Seville. Some 4,000 were slaughtered. Jewish women and children were sold as slaves to Muslims. Many submitted to Christian baptism in order to escape death, while others fled. Some synagogues were turned into churches. Over a three-month period, mob massacres, forced conversions, and suicides spread to many other cities and towns over a large area of Spain. Approximately 70 Jewish communities were attacked.[81]

Because so many Jewish people had been forced to convert to Christianity through baptism, suspicions began to develop that many of these converts were not sincere in their change of faith. Rumors began to circulate that many secretly practiced Judaism. These suspicions and rumors prompted some of the Christian clergy to conclude that some means must be devised to determine if the conversions were true or false. The means was the Inquisition.

In September 1480 the tribunal of the Holy Inquisition was appointed for the city of Seville and its surrounding area, and the Inquisition began to operate in January 1481.[82] All citizens of Seville were commanded, under threat of excommunication, to submit the names of "guilty" Jews to the inquisitors. Among the signs of guilt were (1) belief by a baptized Jew in the future coming of a promised Messiah to administer God's rule over the world; (2) circumcision of children; (3) assignment of Jewish names to children; or (4) following of Jewish dietary laws.

Various means of torture, such as the rack, were used to extract confessions of guilt. The normal means of punishment was burning at a stake and confiscation of property.[83] In some instances, the bodies of suspected "guilty" Jews who died before the Inquisition could do its job were exhumed from their graves and burned.[84]

From 1481 to 1483 the Inquisition existed in Seville, Cadiz, and the Christian province of Andalusia in southern Spain. During that time thousands of victims were burned alive. Others perished in prisons, fled the country, or were made paupers.[85]

But in May 1483 things became worse. Pope Sixtus IV, at the request of King Ferdinand and Queen Isabella, appointed the Dominican prior Tomas de Torquemada as inquisitor-general of Spain. Now almost all of Spain was to be subjected to the horrors of the Inquisition.[86] Many thousands of Jewish people lost their lives throughout Spain.[87]

On March 31, 1492, Ferdinand and Isabella issued a royal

proclamation requiring all Jews who had not converted to Christianity to leave Spain within four months. The only reason given for this decree was that Jewish people were prompting converted Jews to return to Judaism. The expelled Jews were permitted to take only what they could carry with them—but no gold, silver, or money. Any who failed to leave Spain by the deadline would be executed.[88] Despite the presence of the Inquisition, it was hoped that this edict would force many to convert to Christianity and remain in Spain. But few did so. As a result, about 300,000 Jewish people left.[89]

In March 1516, Venice became the first place in Italy to set apart a section of the city as a ghetto for Jewish residents.[90]

In Germany, Martin Luther became extremely anti-Semitic and wished the rulers to persecute Jewish people mercilessly and the preachers to set the mobs against them.

In 1648–1651 in Poland, Greek Orthodox Cossacks from the Ukraine and Little Russia slaughtered many thousands of Jewish people.[91] In 1655 the Cossacks and Russians jointly began a war against Poland. Later Sweden, Prussia, and Transylvania became involved. An estimated 250,000 Jews in Poland were killed by all these forces during this 10-year war.[92]

Haidamak Cossacks from Russia, along with the Turks, attacked Poland and slaughtered many Jews and others from 1768 to 1788.[93]

In 1791 Russia inaugurated the Pale of Settlement. The Pale was described as follows:

A portion of Russia in which Jews are allowed to reside. Unlike other Russian subjects, the Jewish inhabitants do not generally possess the natural right of every citizen to live unrestrictedly in any place in the empire. Furthermore, they are permitted to leave the Pale of Settlement—that is, to move to another place for permanent or for temporary residence—only under certain conditions defined by law.[94]

Nicholas I, czar of Russia from 1825 to 1855, hated the Jewish people because of their faith. He persistently tried to convert them to Orthodox Christianity and regarded most of them as "fanatical, criminal" perpetrators of "evil deeds." As a result, he inflicted harsh, restrictive measures on them.[95]

From 1881 to 1913 several pogroms (government-sanctioned murdering sprees) of vicious repression were carried out against the Jewish people in Russia with the goal of forcing one third to leave, another third to convert to Orthodox Christianity, and the final third to perish.[96] Conditions became so intolerable that approximately 2.6 million Jewish people fled Russia and adjacent countries and migrated to United States.[97]

From 1917 to 1921 there were 887 major pogroms and 349 minor ones against at least 530 Jewish communities in the Ukraine, Poland, Siberia, Mongolia, and Belorussia. Some 60,000 Jewish men, women, and children were massacred and several times that number wounded.[98]

The foundation for the Holocaust of World War II began to be laid in Germany and Austria in the 19th century. Adolf Stoecker, German politician and preacher, started the political anti-Semitic movement in Germany by founding the Social Workers Party in 1878. In 1879 Heinrich von Treitschke, German historian and politician, brought anti-Semitism into intellectual circles; and Wilhelm Marr invented the term "anti-Semitism."[99]

Karl Lueger became mayor of Vienna, Austria, in 1893 and established the anti-Semitic Christian Social party.[100] As a youth, Adolf Hitler listened to Lueger's anti-Semitic views in Vienna.[101]

Adolf Hitler became "fuehrer" of the National Socialist Party in Germany in 1920. His book, *Mein Kampf*, was published in 1925–1927. In 1933 Hitler became chancellor of Germany; an anti-Jewish economic boycott was instituted; and four concentration camps, including Dachau, were prepared.[102] Hitler then used the vicious anti-Semitic statements of Protestant reformer Martin Luther to justify the systematic elimination of millions of Jewish people in the Holocaust of World War II.

On November 9–10, 1938, *Kristallnacht* (Night of Broken Glass) took place. The Nazis viciously attacked Jewish businesses, burned synagogues, and forced Jewish people into concentration camps in Germany and Austria.[103]

World War II began on September 1, 1939, when Germany invaded Poland. Pogroms against the Jewish people swept Poland as the Holocaust began.[104] In 1940 ghettos appeared in Poland. The Nazis shot massive numbers of Jewish people and established the Auschwitz and Belzec extermination camps as they brought Western European Jews under Nazi control.[105]

Germany invaded Russia and the Baltic states in 1941. Pogroms soon followed. More extermination camps were established, and Hitler forced Jewish people from the German Reich into Poland and began deporting and killing the Jews of France. The Nazis also began gassing the Jewish prisoners in extermination camps.[106]

In 1942 a conference in Berlin officially adopted the "Final Solution" program to exterminate all Jews. Hitler began moving large numbers of Jewish people from Belgium and Holland to Auschwitz and had many more slaughtered in Nazi-occupied Russia. Soon he began emptying the ghettos and forcing Jewish people into the death camps. Auschwitz and other camps began to operate at their fullest capacity, and another extermination camp was established.[107]

In 1943 Jewish people from all over Europe, including Italy, were forced into extermination camps; the Warsaw Ghetto and most other ghettos were emptied, and in 1944 Jews in Hungary were eliminated.[108]

On May 8, 1945, Germany surrendered to allied forces; and the Holocaust ended.[109] But by then, close to 6 million Jewish people had perished.

After the war, anti-Semitism continued. In 1946 Jewish people were killed and others wounded in pogroms in Poland. In 1968 severe anti-Semitism broke out again in Poland, and most of the Jewish people in that nation moved elsewhere.[110] In the 1990s a Russian group called Pamyat attempted to prompt a major movement to remove Jewish people and Jewish influences from that nation.

In the opening decade of the 21st century, strident expressions of anti-Semitism have arisen in Western Europe and North America. Large anti-Semitic demonstrations have erupted in major cities in France, where people have burned synagogues and desecrated Jewish cemeteries. Older Jews who managed to survive the Holocaust have warned their children and grandchildren to leave France because they recognize the same types of anti-Semitic activities that took place there in the 1930s. In the United Kingdom, Jewish students are the objects of fierce anti-Semitism from university faculty and students alike.

In the United States significant numbers of neo-Nazi, white supremacist, and other anti-Semitic groups are increasingly using the Internet to spread their hatred. Some college and university professors clearly communicate anti-Semitic concepts and verbally attack Jewish students in the classrooms, and some campuses permit anti-Semitic student organizations and anti-Semitic speeches by visiting speakers.

Even church groups in the United States that are theologically liberal have displayed an anti-Israel bias. In 2003 delegates to the Presbyterian Church USA (PCUSA) general assembly adopted a resolution requesting that the denomination withdraw its shareholding investments from companies that do business with Israel. In addition, in October 2004, 24 representatives of the PCUSA met with leaders of the Hezbollah terrorist group in Lebanon and criticized Israel.[111]

In 2006 the New York Annual Conference of the United Methodist Church also adopted a resolution urging withdrawal of its shareholding investments from companies doing business with Israel and accused Israel of many "illegal and violent activities."[112]

In July 2002 a group of 60 evangelical Christians sent a letter to President George W. Bush asking his administration to alter Middle East policies "tilted in favor of Israel." The letter claimed that

Israel's settlement movement is unlawful and degrading.[113] This contrasted with many evangelical Christians who support Israel's right to exist in the land God gave to it as an everlasting possession and to defend itself against enemies bent on destroying it.

It is important to understand that this list of the effects of Replacement Theology on the Jews is by no means complete. It merely presents survey-fashion samples of the cruel and relentless persecution the Jewish people have endured over a span of approximately 17 centuries.

Conclusion

The Replacement Theology of a major part of organized Christendom is not the only factor that has contributed to anti-Semitism. Islam, some forms of paganism, jealousy, resentment, and false rumors have contributed as well. But it is obvious that Replacement Theology has played an extremely significant role in the unremitting persecution of Jewish people.

A Jewish Perspective. It is interesting to note that Jewish people have recognized the ill effects of Replacement Theology as expressed in the following Jewish statements:

> *The young church, therefore, which declared itself to be the true Israel, or "Israel according to the spirit," heir to the divine promises, found it essential to discredit the "Israel according to the flesh," to prove that God had cast away His people and transferred His love to the Christians. From the outset, therefore, Christian anti-Semitism was an original manifestation: it differed from the traditional tensions between Israel and the nations and did not merely reflect them. Obliged to contest Israel's historic heritage and title, and confronted in addition by a vigorous rabbinical counter-propaganda, the church unremittingly concentrated on the Jews and Judaism.[114]*

> *After Christianity became the official religion of the Roman state (321) the emperors began to translate the concepts and*

claims of the theologians into practice. The ancient privileges granted to the Jews were withdrawn, rabbinical jurisdiction was abolished or severely curtailed, and proselytism was prohibited and made punishable by death, as were relations with Christian women. Finally Jews were excluded from holding high office or pursuing a military career.[115]

The persistence of Judaism, seemingly a contradiction of the Christian conception of the church as the Verus Israel, "the true Israel," led the great theologians, notably Augustine, to elaborate the doctrine that represents the Jews as the nation which was a "witness" to the truth of Christianity. Their existence was further justified by the service they rendered to the Christian truth in attesting through their humiliation the triumph of the church over the synagogue.[116]

Through "allegorization" these early Christian theologians further supported the concept of the triumph of the church over the synagogue by depicting "the Jews as Esau and the Christians as Jacob. . . . Thus the ideological arsenal of Christian anti-Semitism was completely established in antiquity."[117]

It is also interesting to note a Jewish recognition that the apostle Paul in Romans 11 contradicted Replacement Theology. One author wrote that Paul "protests against the idea of God's rejection of the Jews: 'They are beloved for the sake of their forefathers' (Rom. 11:28): 'I myself am an Israelite, a descendant of Abraham, a member of the tribe of Benjamin' (Rom. 11:1)."[118]

The Significance of Romans 11:1–2. In chapter 3 of this book, "Israel and the Abrahamic Covenant," you will see the significance of Paul's statements in Romans 11:28–29. But what about his statements in Romans 11:1–2? In that passage he wrote, "I say then, has God cast away His people? Certainly not! For I also am an Israelite, of the seed of Abraham, of the tribe of Benjamin. God has not cast away His people whom He foreknew."

The word translated "cast away" means "reject, repudiate."[119] Paul was saying that God has not rejected His people Israel.

But what did he mean by *Israel?* Was he referring to Israel as a nation or merely to people spiritually right with God? Four important factors indicate he was referring to Israel as a nation.

(1) Prior to Romans 11, Paul had focused on the nation's sin and its refusal to believe revelation God had given it concerning the Messiah. This rebellion against God, including rejection of God's approach to it through revelation, prompted Paul's question concerning God's response to the nation. Has God rejected it?

(2) Paul used himself as evidence that God had *not* rejected Israel and emphasized his personal relationship to the nation. Like all biological members of the nation, he, too, was an Israelite—a biological descendant of Abraham and a biological member of one of Israel's tribes. The fact that God accepted Paul into right relationship with Him through faith in the Messiah was evidence that God had not rejected Israel as a nation. Apparently, Paul's point was as follows: *If God had rejected Israel as a nation, then He would not have accepted me.*

Certainly the Jewish people of Paul's day knew that, before he became a Christian, Paul, too, had rejected the Messianic revelation God had given the nation. In other words, Paul had been guilty of the same type of rebellion against God as the nation. Thus, if God had rejected the nation of Israel for that rebellion, then certainly He would have rejected Paul also.

(3) Paul described the nation—the supposed object of God's rejection—as "His people" and "His people whom He foreknew." Those descriptions were derived from Old Testament passages that refer to the entire nation of Israel, not merely to a faithful remnant.

Some passages indicate that God elected the nation of Israel to be, in a unique sense, His people forever. Moses told the nation of Israel, "You are a holy people to the LORD your God; the LORD your God has chosen you to be a people for Himself, a special treasure above all the peoples on the face of the earth" (Dt. 7:6).

King David wrote the following:

> *And who is like Your people, like Israel, the one nation on the earth whom God went to redeem for Himself as a people, to make for Himself a name—and to do for Yourself great and awesome deeds for Your land—before Your people whom You redeemed for Yourself from Egypt, the nations and their gods? For You have made Your people Israel Your very own people forever; and You, LORD, have become their God* (2 Sam. 7:23–24).

Other passages clearly assert that God will *never* reject the nation of Israel as His people. To a generation of Israelites who had just sinned against God, Samuel said, "For the LORD will not forsake His people, for His great name's sake, because it has pleased the LORD to make you His people" (1 Sam. 12:22). Psalm 94:14 declares, "For the LORD will not cast off His people, nor will He forsake His inheritance." In Jeremiah 31:37 God indicated that the only way He would "cast off all the seed of Israel for all that they have done" is if mankind could do what is impossible.

(4) In light of Paul's strong response ("Certainly not!"), William Sanday and Arthur C. Headlam wrote the following concerning the expression *His people whom He foreknew:*

> *The addition of these words gives a reason for the emphatic denial of which they form a part. Israel was the race which God in His Divine foreknowledge had elected and chosen, and therefore He could not cast it off. The reference in this chapter is throughout to the election of the nation as a whole, and therefore the words cannot have a limiting sense (Orig. Chrys. Aug.), "that people whom He foreknew," i.e. those of His people whom He foreknew; nor again can they possibly refer to the spiritual Israel, as that would oblige a meaning to be given to laos [people] different from that in ver. 1.*[120]

The verb translated "cast away" in the question "has God cast away His people?" (Rom. 11:1) is in the middle voice. It appears to be the indirect middle that "lays stress upon the agent as producing the action" and "signifies that the action is closely related to the subject, or is related to the subject in some special and distinctive sense which the writer wishes to emphasize."[121] So the force of the question is as follows: "Has God Himself cast away His people?" This distinction is significant.

- First, one of the reasons God chose the nation of Israel to be His unique people is because He swore a solemn oath to Israel's ancestors—Abraham, Isaac, and Jacob—to keep the promises He had established in the Abrahamic Covenant with them and their biological descendants (Ex. 32:13; Dt. 7:6–8). Thus the nation's unique relationship with God as His people is tied to that covenant, which He declared to be everlasting (Gen. 17:7–8, 19).

- Second, since God made all the commitments in that covenant, and the nation of Israel made none, then God *Himself* is the only party of that covenant who could break it.

- Third, since God *Himself* is the only party who could break the covenant, then the covenant remaining in effect and the nation of Israel remaining His unique people depends totally on God *Himself* being faithful to His oath to keep His promises.

- Fourth, since the covenant remaining in effect and the nation of Israel remaining His unique people depends totally on God *Himself* being faithful to His oath to keep His promises, then if God *Himself* were to cast away or reject the nation of Israel as His people, that would mean that God is not faithful to keep His promises.

Because the very idea that God is not faithful to keep His promises was so repulsive to Paul, his response to the question "Has God cast away His people?" was "the most emphatic negative available."[122] It literally said, "May it not be."[123]

An Important Distinction. It is important to note that the Bible uses the terms *elect* and *chosen* in two distinct ways: collectively and individually. In fact, Paul used the terminology in those two distinct ways in Romans 11. First, he "uses the term for the election of all Israel in the fathers, R. 11:28. . . . Here the reference is not to a part (cf. R. 9:11; 11:5, 7) but to the whole people."[124] This refers to God electing, or choosing, all of Israel collectively, including saved and unsaved people, to have a unique relationship with Him as a nation. This type of election was not related to the spiritual salvation of individuals. As "King of the nations," God often works out His sovereign purposes through nations. God sovereignly elected, or chose, the nation of Israel to have a unique relationship with Him so that Israel would become a special instrument through which He would accomplish major aspects of His sovereign plan and purpose for history. It is in that sense, not in a personal-salvation sense, that Israel is the elect, or Chosen People, of God. The fact that the accomplishment of some of those major aspects of God's purpose through Israel is yet future indicates that God has not cast away the nation of Israel as His people.

In Romans 11:5 Paul employed the second distinct way in which the terms *elect* and *chosen* are used in the Bible. There he referred to "a remnant according to the election of grace." This refers to "God's selecting of a part of Israel out of the whole. . . . This remnant of Christian believers in Israel is chosen according to the principle of grace." It is "the selection of a part from the whole—Israel as a national community—to a place of privilege."[125] This type of election is related to the spiritual salvation of individuals.

Paul's statements in Romans 11:1–2 completely contradict Replacement Theology. To say that, because the nation of Israel as a whole does not recognize Jesus as its Messiah, then God has forever rejected the nation of Israel as His unique people and has replaced it with the church, is to say that God is not faithful to keep His promises. If God cannot be trusted to keep His promises to Israel, then how can Christians trust Him to keep His promises to us individually and to the body of Christ, the church?

ENDNOTES

[1] Kenneth Scott Latourette, *The First Five Centuries*, Vol. 1 of *A History of the Expansion of Christianity* (Grand Rapids: Zondervan, 1970), 70.

[2] Ibid., 83.

[3] Ibid.

[4] Ibid., 70–71.

[5] Ibid., 71–72.

[6] Ibid., 74.

[7] Ibid.

[8] Ibid., 83.

[9] Ibid., 84.

[10] Ibid.

[11] Adolph Harnack, *The Mission and Expansion of Christianity in the First Three Centuries*, 2nd ed. trans./ed. James Moffatt (New York: G. P. Putnam's Sons, 1908), 1:69; quoted in Latourette, 84.

[12] *Ante-Nicene Fathers*, ed. Alexander Roberts and James Donaldson (Peabody, MA: Hendrickson, 1994), 1:267.

[13] Ibid.

[14] Ibid., 3:151–152.

[15] Philip Schaff, *History of the Christian Church* (Grand Rapids: Eerdmans, 1973), 2:791.

[16] Ibid., 2:792

[17] Adolph Harnack, "Millennium," *The Encyclopedia Britannica*, 9th ed. (New York: Charles Scribner's Sons, 1883), XVI, 316.

[18] *Ante-Nicene Fathers*, 5:507.

[19] Ibid., 512.

[20] Ibid., 514.

[21] Schaff, 3:940.

[22] *The Jewish Encyclopedia* (New York: Funk and Wagnalls, 1907), s.v. "Chrysostom, Cyril, and Ambrose," 4:82.

[23] For a thorough, scholarly treatment of this subject, read Ronald E. Diprose, *ISRAEL in the Development of Christian Thought* (Rome: Istituto Biblico Evangelico Italiano, 2000).

[24] Ibid., 105–140 (in-depth treatment of these ecclesiastical changes).

[25] Harnack, "Millennium," XVI, 316.

[26] Ibid.

[27] Ibid.

[28] Ibid., 317.

[29] Ibid.

[30] Diprose, 93.

[31] Ibid.

[32] Ibid., 94.

[33] Ernest R. Sandeen, "Millennialism," *The Encyclopaedia Britannica*, 15th ed. (Chicago: Encyclopaedia Britannica, 1974), 12, 202.

[34] Augustine, *The City of God*, book 20, chap. 6, trans. Marcus Dods (New York: Random House, 1950), 717.

[35] Harnack, "Millennium," XVI, 317.

[36] Augustine, book 20, chap. 9, 725.

[37] Ibid., 725–726.

[38] Sandeen.

[39] Harnack, "Millennium," XVI, 317.

[40] For in-depth treatment of these changes in eschatology, see Diprose, 153–174.

[41] Harnack, "Millennium," XVI, 318.

[42] Ibid.

[43] *The Jewish Encyclopedia*, s.v. "Luther, Martin," 8:213.

[44] Ibid., 214.

[45] Ibid., 215.

[46] Charles Caldwell Ryrie, *Dispensationalism Today* (Chicago: Moody Press, 1965), 179.

[47] *The Jewish Encyclopedia*, s.v. "Constantine I," 4:236.

[48] Ibid.

[49] Ibid.

[50] Heinrich Graetz, *History of the Jews* (Philadelphia: Jewish Publication Society of America, 1893), 2:562.

[51] Latourette, 1:181.

[52] Graetz, 617.

[53] Ibid., 618–619.

[54] Ibid., 3:12–17.

[55] Kenneth Scott Latourette, *The Thousand Years of Uncertainty*, Vol. 2 of *A History of the Expansion of Christianity* (Grand Rapids: Zondervan, 1970), 229.

[56] Graetz, 3:46.

[57] Ibid., 40.

[58] Latourette, 2:215.

[59] Graetz, 3:122–123.

[60] Ibid., 3:161–171.

[61] Ibid., 3:245–246.

[62] Ibid., 3:293.

[63] Ibid.

[64] Ibid., 3:294, quoted by Graetz; original source not given.

[65] *The Jewish Encyclopedia*, s.v. "Crusades, The," 4:378.

[66] Ibid.

[67] Graetz, 3:496.

[68] Ibid., 3:500.

[69] Ibid., 3:498–501.

[70] Ibid., 3:511.

[71] Ibid., 3:401.

[72] Ibid., 3:402.

[73] Ibid.

[74] Ibid., 3:403.

[75] Ibid., 3:404.

[76] Ibid., 3:642–646.

[77] *The Jewish Encyclopedia*, s.v. "Rindfleisch," 10:427.

[78] Graetz, 3:610–611.

[79] Ibid., 4:97–98.

[80] Ibid., 4:100–112.

[81] Ibid., 4:166–173.

[82] Ibid., 4:312–313.

[83] Ibid., 4:314–316.

[84] Ibid., 4:318.

[85] Ibid., 4:323.

[86] Ibid., 4:323–325.

[87] Ibid., 4:332.

[88] Ibid., 4:347.

[89] Ibid., 4:350–352.

[90] Ibid., 4:408.

[91] Ibid., 5:1–14.

[92] Ibid., 5:14–15.

[93] Ibid., 5:388.

[94] *The Jewish Encyclopedia*, s.v. "Pale of Settlement," 9:468.

[95] Ibid., s.v. "Russia," 10:523–526.

[96] Ibid., 10:526–528.

[97] Rabbi Arthur Hertzberg, "Ideological Evolution," *Zionism*, in Israel Pocket Library Series (Jerusalem: Keter Publishing, 1973), 20–21.

[98] Prof. Yehuda Slutsky, "Pogroms," *Anti-Semitism*, in Israel Pocket Library Series (Jerusalem: Keter Publishing, 1974), 131–134.

[99] "Chronology," Ibid., 208.

[100] Ibid., 209.

[101] "Anti-Semitism," Ibid., 40.

[102] "Chronology," Ibid., 210.

[103] Ibid.

[104] Ibid., 211.

[105] Ibid.

[106] Ibid.

[107] Ibid.

[108] Ibid., 211–212.

[109] Ibid., 212.

[110] Ibid.

[111] Edward E. Plowman, "Taking stock," *World*, November 13, 2004, p. 33.

[112] Mark D. Tooley, "Methodists for MoveOn," *Front Page Magazine*, August 4, 2006 <frontpagemag.com/Articles/Read.aspx?GUID=16961A5E-AED5-436D-B25B-76BF398FE4AF>.

[113] Eli Kintisch, "An Evangelical Group Faults U.S. Tilt Toward Israel" *Forward*, September 13, 2002.

[114] "Anti-Semitism," *Anti-Semitism,* Ibid., 12.

[115] Ibid., 13.

[116] Ibid.

[117] Ibid.

[118] Ibid., 11.

[119] William F. Arndt and F. Wilbur Gingrich, eds./trans., "apotheo" *A Greek English Lexicon of the New Testament and Other Early Christian Literature* (1952: translation and adaptation of Walter Bauer's *Griechisch-Deutsches Worterbuch zu den Schriften des Neuen Testaments und der ubrigen urchristlichen Literatur,* 4th ed.; Chicago: University of Chicago Press, 1957), 102–103.

[120] William Sanday and Arthur C. Headlam, *A Critical and Exegetical Commentary on the Epistle to the Romans,* 5th ed. (Edinburgh: T. & T. Clark, 1958), 310.

[121] H. E. Dana and Julius R. Mantey, *A Manual Grammar of the Greek New Testament* (New York: Macmillan, 1955), 158–159.

[122] John Murray, *The Epistle to the Romans* in *The New International Commentary on the New Testament* (Grand Rapids: Eerdmans, 1965), 66.

[123] Arndt and Gingrich, "ginomai," 157.

[124] G. Schrenk, "ekloge," *Theological Dictionary of the New Testament,* ed. Gerhard Kittel, trans./ed. Geoffrey W. Bromiley, translated from *Theologisches Worterbuch zum Neuen Testament* (Grand Rapids: Eerdmans, 1967), 4:179.

[125] Ibid., 180.

CHAPTER 2

ISRAEL AND GOD

Many people who adhere to Replacement Theology fail to understand God's unique relationship with Israel and His purpose for the nation. God did not choose Israel because He considered it better than others. Nor did He choose it because of its size, its spirituality, the intellect of its people, or any other such reason. These are fallacious human arguments that have no basis in God's Word. When Israel's place in God's plan is understood properly, it becomes easy to see why God would never replace Israel with the church and why Israel in the future will play a key role in fulfilling God's purpose for history.

Israel's Unique Relationship With God

In ancient days, God's appointed leader of Israel, the prophet Moses, made an extremely significant statement to the generation of Jewish people who survived the 40 years of wilderness wandering after Israel's Exodus from Egypt. This was the generation that, in obedience to God's command, would soon conquer the land of Canaan that God had sworn to give the descendants of Abraham, Isaac, and Jacob (Dt. 6:18–19).

"You are a holy people to the LORD your God," said Moses. "The LORD your God has chosen you to be a people for Himself, a special treasure above all the peoples on the face of the earth" (7:6). The root meaning of the word translated "holy" is "to divide."[1] To be holy is to be divided from other people or things in the sense of being different from them, distinct, or unique. God had divided the people of Israel from all other people, setting them apart to have a unique relationship with Him that would be unlike His relationship with any other nation.

There are two important facts about this unique relationship. First, as we said earlier, God established it with the entire nation of Israel, which included both the saved and unsaved. Second, this relationship is permanent. King David, who claimed that the Spirit of the Lord spoke by him and that God's Word was on his tongue (2 Sam. 23:2), spoke the following concerning God:

> *And who is like Your people, like Israel, the one nation on the earth whom God went to redeem for Himself as a people, to make for Himself a name—and to do for Yourself great and awesome deeds for Your land—before Your people whom You redeemed for Yourself from Egypt, the nations, and their gods? For You have made Your people Israel Your very own people forever; and You, LORD, have become their God (7:23–24).*

Because God chose Israel for this unique relationship with Him, He called Israel "My elect" (Isa. 45:4).

The Basis of This Relationship

God did not choose Israel because of its size. Moses told the Israelites, "The LORD did not set His love on you nor choose you because you were more in number than any other people, for you were the least of all peoples" (Dt. 7:7). The basis of God's choice was twofold.

First, God earlier had made Israel's ancestors—Abraham, Isaac, and Jacob—the objects of His love. Because God loved these men, He chose their biological descendants—the people of Israel—for this unique relationship. Moses told the nation,

> *And because He loved your fathers, therefore He chose their descendants after them; and He brought you out of Egypt with His Presence, with His mighty power, driving out from before you nations greater and mightier than you, to bring you in, to give you their land as an inheritance, as it is this day. The*

*LORD delighted only in your fathers, to love them; and He chose
their descendants after them, you above all peoples, as it is this
day* (Dt. 4:37–38; 10:15).

Second, Moses told the people of Israel that God also chose the
nation "because He would keep the oath which He swore to your
fathers" (7:8). Exodus 32:13 sheds light on that oath. In that passage
Moses said to God, "Remember Abraham, Isaac, and Israel, Your
servants, to whom you swore by Your own self, and said to them,
'I will multiply your descendants as the stars of heaven; and all
this land that I have spoken of I give to your descendants, and
they shall inherit it forever'" (*Israel* here refers to Jacob [see Genesis
32:28]).

Moses' statement refers to two promises of the Abrahamic
Covenant. When God established that covenant with Abraham,
Isaac, and Jacob, He swore a solemn oath to keep the covenant's
promises. Thus God chose to have a permanent, unique relationship
with the nation of Israel—the physical descendants of Abraham,
Isaac, and Jacob—in order to keep His promise to (1) multiply
greatly those descendants and (2) give them a "forever" inheritance
of the land of Canaan.

God's Unique Purposes for Israel

The fact that God established this unique relationship with
Israel means He has sovereign purposes for the nation. The Bible
reveals at least three.

To Glorify Himself Through Israel. After God indicated
that He "formed" Israel (Isa. 43:1), He declared that He "created"
the nation for His "glory" (v. 7): "This people I have formed for
Myself; they shall declare My praise" (v. 21). Isaiah 44:23 says that
God has "glorified Himself in Israel" and called the nation "Israel
My glory" (46:13).

Someone's "glory" is whatever is impressive or influential about
that individual. The Hebrew text of Genesis 31:1 uses the word
that means "glory" to describe Jacob's great wealth, indicating it

was Jacob's wealth that impressed people with Jacob and gave him influence. Joseph's powerful position in the Egyptian government is called his "glory" (Gen. 45:13). It was that position that impressed people with Joseph and gave him influence. Thus God's glory is whatever is impressive or influential concerning God. That God has purposed to glorify Himself through Israel indicates He intends, through that nation, to so impress the world with who He is and how great He is that He will have life-changing influence on multitudes of people.

How does God manifest His glory through Israel? The Bible says He does it through His historic dealings with the nation. In Deuteronomy 28—30 God revealed to Israel the twofold way He would deal with it throughout history from Moses' time onward: He would bless the nation for obedience and curse it for disobedience. If the nation obeyed God's Word that was given to it, God would bless it abundantly (Dt. 28:1–14). Moses told the Israelites,

> *Now it shall come to pass, if you diligently obey the voice of the LORD your God, to observe carefully all His commandments which I command you today, that the LORD your God will set you high above all nations of the earth. And all these blessings shall come upon you and overtake you, because you obey the voice of the LORD your God* (vv. 1–2).

After listing the blessings, Moses continued: "And the LORD will make you the head and not the tail; you shall be above only, and not beneath, if you heed the commandments of the LORD your God, which I command you today, and are careful to observe them" (v. 13).

But if the nation disobeyed, God would curse it severely (vv. 15–68). "But it shall come to pass," Moses warned, "if you do not obey the voice of the LORD your God, to observe carefully all His commandments and His statutes which I command you today, that all these curses will come upon you and overtake you" (v. 15). Then Moses enumerated a long list of curses.

One involved God scattering Israel from its homeland:

Then the LORD will scatter you among all peoples, from one end of the earth to the other. . . . And among those nations you shall find no rest, nor shall the sole of your foot have a resting place; but there the LORD will give you a trembling heart, failing eyes, and anguish of soul (vv. 64–65).

Over the centuries many Jewish people have been forced to wander from nation to nation.

Moses also told them what they would experience while scattered:

Your life shall hang in doubt before you; you shall fear day and night, and have no assurance of life. In the morning you shall say, "Oh, that it were evening!" And at evening you shall say, "Oh, that it were morning!" because of the fear that terrifies your heart, and because of the sight which your eyes see (vv. 66–67).

These solemn words describe what millions of Jewish people who were scattered among the European nations experienced in the Holocaust. Before World War II, the world Jewish population was approximately 17 million. In fewer than 10 years, more than one-third of that population was systematically exterminated from the earth. Terror gripped the hearts of all the Jews in Europe, particularly those in concentration camps. Faced with torture and death, they despaired of life itself. In the morning they did not know what fate awaited them or if they would survive until evening. And when evening came, they did not know if they would be alive the next morning.

Why would God deal with Israel in this twofold way? Why would He bless it more than any other nation when it would obey Him and curse it when it did not? Deuteronomy 28:10 answers that question: "Then all peoples of the earth shall see that you are called by the name of the LORD." God's intent was for other nations to see that Israel was more blessed than they, causing them to investigate why this was so. Then they would discover that it was because of Israel's relationship with the true and living God: Israel received revelation of truth from God and obeyed it.

However, if Israel failed to heed God's Word, God would curse it: "And you shall become an astonishment, a proverb, and a byword among all nations where the LORD will drive you" (v. 37). The word translated "astonishment" refers to "shock" or "horror" that people experience when they witness the devastation that divine judgment has brought on another party.[2] The word translated "proverb" refers to "a public example" or "object lesson" to other people.[3] God purposed that, when other nations saw Israel being cursed with devastating divine judgment, they would be so shocked or horrified that they would consider what lesson they should learn from Israel's experience.

Moses indicated that God manifests His glory through Israel by making that nation a public example or object lesson to the rest of the world. His twofold way of dealing historically with Israel is designed to impress mankind with two great truths concerning Himself so that He can have life-changing influence on multitudes of people: (1) He will bless people who obey His revealed Word that He has given to mankind. (2) He will curse with judgment those who do not.

In light of this purpose for Israel, it is no mistake that God placed that nation in the most strategic geographic location on the face of the earth. Israel is the crossroads of three of the world's great continents: Africa, Asia, and Europe. Because of its key location, ancient nations called that land "the navel of the earth." Back then people who traveled between these continents by land had to travel through Israel. They would have observed firsthand either the blessing or cursing of Israel and been personally impacted by what they saw.

In addition, in light of this purpose for Israel, it is no mistake that God restored it as a nation in 1948 in that same strategic location and has enabled it to exist there despite many attempts by determined and powerful enemies to eliminate it. And it is no mere coincidence that the world's attention continues to be drawn to Israel almost daily in a way that is completely disproportionate to Israel's size.

Prophetic portions of the Bible indicate that some of the greatest manifestations of God's glory through Israel are yet to come in conjunction with the seven-year Tribulation, Second Coming of Christ, and Millennial reign of Christ.

To Bless All Families of the Earth Through Israel. God promised Abraham, "And in you all the families of the earth shall be blessed" (Gen. 12:3). Later God delivered the same promise in enlarged form to Jacob, Abraham's grandson, "and in you and in your seed all the families of the earth shall be blessed" (28:14). This blessing comes not merely through Jacob, but also through his "seed," the people of Israel.

Jacob fathered 12 sons, and those men became the heads of the 12 tribes of Israel. Thus, through this promise of the Abrahamic Covenant, God revealed His purpose to bless all the world through the nation of Israel. He already has brought several significant blessings to mankind through Israel.

The divinely inspired record of truth that God revealed to mankind came through Israel. The apostle Paul referred to this fact in Romans 3:1–2. After asking, "What advantage then has the Jew, or what is the profit of circumcision?" he responded, "Much in every way! Chiefly because to them were committed the oracles of God."

Concerning the expression *the oracles of God,* John Murray indicated that the Jewish people "were the depositories of God's special revelation."[4] He stated further,

> *(1) Paul is undoubtedly thinking of the Old Testament in its entirety. . . . (2) It is as Scripture that these oracles were committed to the Jews; only in this form could the Jews be said to have been entrusted with them. (3) The deposit of revelation in the Scripture of the Old Testament is called "the oracles of God." . . . For Paul the written Word is God's speech, and God's speech is conceived of as existing in the form*

of a "trust" to Israel; divine oracles have fixed and abiding form. . . . When we think of what, above all else, was the Jew's privilege as an abiding possession it was his entrustment with the Word of God.[5]

But it wasn't just the Old Testament that God gave to mankind through Israel; He also gave the New Testament. All the books of the New Testament, with the possible exception of the Gospel According to Luke and the Acts of the Apostles, were written by Jewish men. (Some New Testament scholars are now beginning to think Luke may have been Jewish rather than Gentile.) Thus the Bible, God's written Word, that over several millennia has brought great blessing to multitudes of people from many backgrounds and areas of the world, came to mankind through Israel.

God also provided for mankind's salvation from eternal judgment through Israel by sending His Son to the world through the Jewish nation. In eternity past the divine decision was made for God's Son to come to Earth and become a human being through incarnation so that He could provide salvation for mankind. Centuries before His Son came, God revealed that He would give His Son to the world ("Unto us a Son is given," Isa. 9:6) and that His Son would be incarnated as a human being through birth ("For unto us a Child is born," v. 6).

Since God's Son was to become incarnated (meaning He "became flesh," Jn. 1:14), His birth would have to come through some nation. God chose Israel to be that nation. Thus, several centuries before that birth, God revealed that His Son would be born in the Israelite town of Bethlehem: "But you, Bethlehem Ephrathah, though you are little among the thousands of Judah, yet out of you shall come forth to Me the One to be Ruler in Israel, whose goings forth are from of old, from everlasting" (Mic. 5:2).

When the time was right for these divine revelations to be fulfilled, God sent the angel Gabriel to a betrothed Jewish virgin named Mary in the Israelite city of Nazareth (Lk. 1:26–27). The angel informed Mary that, as a result of the Holy Spirit supernaturally causing her to conceive, she would give birth to a holy Son, a biological descendant of Israel's King David. That Son was to have the human name of Jesus, but He would also be called the Son of God (vv. 28–35). Months later Mary gave birth to Jesus in the city of Bethlehem (2:1–7). That night an angel announced Jesus' birth to shepherds in fields near Bethlehem, identifying Him as "Savior" and "Christ [Messiah]" (vv. 8–12).

Thus God's Son, Jesus Christ, derived His humanity through Israel. The apostle Paul emphasized this fact when he indicated that the Israelites, his "countrymen according to the flesh," were the ones "from whom, according to the flesh, Christ came, who is over all" (Rom. 9:3, 5).

The angel's identification of Jesus as "Savior" indicated God gave His Son to the world to become a human being in order to be the Savior of mankind. As a result of becoming human, Jesus made salvation from eternal judgment for sin available to human beings by taking their judgment as their sacrificial substitute when He died on the cross. Thus an angel told Joseph, His stepfather, "You shall call His name JESUS, for He will save His people from their sins" (Mt. 1:21).

John the Baptist said of Jesus, "Behold! The Lamb of God who takes away the sin of the world!" (Jn. 1:29). The apostle Paul wrote, "But when the fullness of the time had come, God sent forth His Son, born of a woman, born under the law, to redeem those who were under the law" (Gal. 4:4–5). Paul also stated that God "made Him who knew no sin to be sin for us, that we might become the righteousness of God in Him" (2 Cor. 5:21). The writer of the Epistle to the Hebrews declared, "Inasmuch then as the children have partaken of flesh and blood, He Himself likewise shared in the same. . . . Therefore, in all things He had to be made like His brethren, that He might be a merciful and faithful High Priest in things pertaining to God, to make propitiation for the sins of the people" (2:14, 17). The apostle Peter said Jesus "Himself bore our sins in His own body on the tree" (1 Pet. 2:24), and "Christ also suffered once for sins, the just for the unjust, that He might bring us to God, being put to death in the flesh but made alive by the Spirit" (3:18).

The apostle John focused on God's motive for giving His Son to the world:

> *For God so loved the world that He gave His only begotten Son, that whoever believes in Him should not perish but have everlasting life. For God did not send His Son into the world to condemn the world, but that the world through Him might be saved. He who believes in Him is not condemned; but he who does not believe is condemned already, because he has not believed in the name of the only begotten Son of God* (Jn. 3:16–18).

God loved lost mankind so much that He gave His Son to be our Savior, our sacrificial substitute, who took in full our punishment for sin so that all who place their trust in Him can be saved from eternal condemnation. Since it was through Israel that God's Son obtained the humanity that enabled Him to become that sacrificial substitute, one of the blessings God gave all families of the earth through Israel is salvation. Jesus Himself said so when He told the Samaritan woman at Jacob's well, "Salvation is of the Jews" (Jn. 4:22).

Mankind also has been blessed abundantly through the medical research conducted by the biological descendants of Israel. Jewish medical personnel scattered among the nations have contributed immeasurably to medical advancements. Following is just a smattering of what they have discovered or developed: effective testing for and treatment of syphilis, a method for measuring blood pressure, a cure for beriberi, the concept of vitamins, a vaccine for cholera, ophthalmological instruments for examining human eyes, the laryngoscope for examining the human larynx, polio vaccines, a method to discern susceptibility to diphtheria, various antibiotics, the original and effective medicine for tuberculosis, a method for diagnosing and preventing typhoid fever, insulin, the relationship of diabetes and the pancreas, knowledge of different blood types, and cortisone.[6]

To Play a Key Role in Fulfilling His Purpose for History. In eternity past, the personal, sovereign God of the Bible decided to create a universal Kingdom over which He could rule as sovereign King. God created the universe, consisting of "the heavens and the earth, the sea, and all that is in them" as the realm of His universal Kingdom (Ex. 20:11). He also created two types of personal subjects to serve Him: angels and people. First, He created an enormous host of angels with different degrees of intelligence and power to serve Him primarily in the heavenly realm of His universal Kingdom (Ps. 103:19–22; 148:2–5). Then God created man and gave him dominion over the earthly province of His universal Kingdom (Gen. 1:26–28).

The original form of government that God established for Earth was a theocracy. In a theocracy, God's rule is administered through a representative. God appointed the first man, Adam, to be His representative on the earth. As God's representative, it was Adam's responsibility to administer God's rule over the entire earthly province of God's universal Kingdom in the way God wanted it to be administered.

After God finished creating His universal Kingdom, He evaluated everything He had made and pronounced it "very good" (v. 31). But it did not remain that way long. Soon the highest-ranked, most magnificent angel God created—"the anointed cherub who covers," who was "perfect" in his ways from the day he was created until "iniquity was found" in him (Ezek. 28:14–15)—became consumed with pride (v. 17; 1 Tim. 3:6). He began a war against God aimed at overthrowing God from His position as sovereign Ruler of the universe. Determined to usurp that position for himself, he boasted, "I will be like the Most High" (Isa. 14:14). He thereby became Satan, the great adversary, or enemy, of God.

After Satan prompted other angels to join him in his revolt (Mt. 25:41; Rev. 12:2–9), he persuaded Adam to rebel against God (Gen. 3:1–12). As a result of God's human representative defecting from God, the earthly theocracy was lost. By joining Satan's war, Adam handed over the rule of the world system to God's great enemy; and Satan and his forces have been dominating the world system ever since (Lk. 4:5–7; Jn. 14:30; 1 Jn. 5:19).

Since the goal of Satan's war against God is to overthrow God from His position as sovereign Ruler of the universe and usurp that position for himself, God's purpose for history is to glorify Himself by demonstrating that He alone is the sovereign God of the universe. The Bible reveals that, in order for God to accomplish that purpose for history, there are certain things He must do before the history of this present earth ends. First, God must crush Satan and eliminate him and his evil rule of the world system. Second, after He crushes Satan, God must restore His theocracy to the earth. Doing so would require another Adam, a human representative, administering God's rule over the entire earth for the last age of its history. If God did not accomplish these things before the history of the present earth ends, then God would end up defeated by His enemy Satan within the scope of the present earth's history.

Immediately after Adam joined Satan's war, God informed His enemy that, during the course of history, a man-child born of a woman would crush him (Gen. 3:15). Later God began to reveal that the promised Redeemer would be born of a woman through Israel. Jesus Christ is that Redeemer. He was born of a Jewish woman, the virgin Mary, in the Israelite city of Bethlehem. Since the Redeemer (God's key to Satan's defeat) was born through Israel, that nation has played a key role in God's fulfillment of His purpose for history.

But Israel's role is not finished. The Bible indicates that it will play another key role in God's fulfillment of His purpose for history. According to Zechariah 12—14, Jesus Christ the Redeemer will not crush Satan and his forces, rid the earth of them, and restore God's theocracy to the earth until the nation of Israel repents of its rebellion against God. When it does so, it will become reconciled to Jesus as its Messiah and Savior. It is exclusively Israel, not the Gentiles or Samaritans, that must be reconciled to God before God's purpose for history will be fulfilled.

The leaders and armies of all nations will invade Israel in an attempt to destroy it (Zech. 12:1–3; cf. Rev. 16:12–16). Two-thirds of the Jewish people there will perish (Zech. 13:8). The third that remains will be surrounded and attacked (14:2). When its defeat is near and there is no nation it can appeal to for help, Israel will realize that God alone is its sole hope for survival. At that moment, all Israel will turn to Him with all its heart, cease trusting in itself and its allies, and cry out for Him to send the Messiah (13:9). In response, God will deliver them by sending the resurrected and glorified Redeemer, Jesus Christ, from heaven.

Zechariah 12:10 says, "They will look on Me whom they pierced. Yes, they will mourn for Him as one mourns for his only son, and grieve for Him as one grieves for a firstborn." When God's ancient people see the resurrected, glorified Messiah descend from heaven with the wounds of His crucifixion in His resurrection body, they recognize Him and repent. The word *repent* refers to a change of mind. They will change their minds about Him and accept Him as their Messiah and Savior. God will respond by cleansing them of their sin (13:1).

Then Christ will go to battle and fight for Israel. He will destroy the leaders and armies of all the nations of the world (14:3–4, 11–15; cf. Rev. 19:11–21). He also will bind Satan and imprison him in the bottomless pit for 1,000 years (Rev. 20:1–3). Then Christ will restore God's theocracy to the earth and, as God's representative (the last Adam), administer God's rule over all the earthly province of God's universal Kingdom for 1,000 years on this present earth and forever on the new, eternal earth (Isa. 9:6–7; Dan. 7:13–14; Zech. 14:9, 16–21; Lk. 1:30–33; 1 Cor. 15:45; Rev. 20:4–6).

Then God will have fulfilled His purpose for history. He will have glorified Himself by demonstrating that He alone is the sovereign God of the universe.

Why Is Israel So Important? Through Old Testament prophets God revealed that in the future, restored theocracy, the nation of Israel will be the spiritual leader of the world. God reserved this position for Israel alone; it is not for any other nation. Since a spiritual leader who is in rebellion against God cannot lead others into a right relationship with Him, it is crucial that Israel be reconciled to its Messiah. God will not crush Satan or restore His theocracy until the nation that is to be the spiritual leader of the world is itself in a right relationship with Him.

Where in the prophets did God reveal that Israel is to be the spiritual leader of the world in the theocracy? Isaiah 2:1–4 says that, during the theocracy, Christ will dwell in God's Temple in Jerusalem, Israel's capital city. People of all nations will come to Jerusalem to hear God's Word and be instructed concerning how Christ will administer God's theocratic rule over them. Therefore, during the theocracy, Israel's capital city will not only be the world's governmental center, but also its spiritual center.

In addition, Isaiah 61:6 says the Jewish people will "be named the priests of the Lord," and the Gentiles will call them "the servants of our God." And Zechariah 8:20–23 says people from many cities and nations will go to Jerusalem to pray and seek the Lord (vv. 20–22). "In those days ten men from every language of the nations shall grasp the sleeve of a Jewish man, saying, 'Let us go with you, for we have heard that God is with you'" (v. 23).

Satan, of course, hates Israel. If he could destroy Israel before it turned to the Messiah, then he would win his battle with God. Christ would never crush him, and God would never fulfill His purpose for history. Consequently, Satan wants desperately to destroy Israel. This fact explains why more attempts at genocide have been brought against the Jewish people than any other ethnic group in the world. The Holocaust of World War II is a prime example. This is why Israel has so many enemies that are determined to eliminate it. This is why all nations will come against Israel right before Christ will return to Earth. (See Revelation 16:12–16.)

And this is why Israel in the future will play a key role in fulfilling God's purpose for history.

ENDNOTES

[1] Otto Proksch, "hagios," *Theological Dictionary of the New Testament*, ed. Gerhard Kittel, ed./trans. Geoffrey W. Bromiley, translated from *Theologisches Worterbuch zum Neuen Testament* (Grand Rapids: Eerdmans, 1964), 1:89.

[2] Hermann J. Austel, "shamem," *Theological Wordbook of the Old Testament* (hereafter cited as *TWOT*), ed. R. Laird Harris, Gleason L. Archer Jr., and Bruce K. Waltke (Chicago: Moody Press, 1980), 2:936–937.

[3] Victor P. Hamilton, "mashal," *TWOT,* 1:533.

[4] John Murray, *The Epistle to the Romans* (Grand Rapids: Eerdmans, 1965), 1:92.

[5] Ibid., 92–93.

[6] Lorna Simcox, "Jews Who Made a Difference," *Israel My Glory* 51, no. 2 (1993): 19–20, 15.

CHAPTER 3

ISRAEL AND THE ABRAHAMIC COVENANT

The Arab-Israeli conflict has grown to massive proportions. And there are evangelical Christians on both sides of the issue. Replacement theologians tend to side with the Palestinians, while dispensationalists tend to side with Israel. The key question in this conflict is this: Who rightfully owns the land where the State of Israel exists? The Jewish people or the Muslims?

Islam teaches that once Muslims have subjugated an area of the world to Islamic rule, that area belongs irrevocably to Allah forever. If a non-Muslim force should succeed in removing Islamic rule from that area, Allah is dishonored. Thus, for the sake of Allah, the non-Muslims must be eliminated and Islamic rule restored at any cost, even if it requires killing many innocent people and losing many Muslim lives.

During the Middle Ages and later, Muslim forces several times subjugated and ruled the land Israel had owned and inhabited for many centuries. The last of those forces was the Turkish Ottoman Empire that ruled the land for some 400 years until Great Britain defeated Turkey during World War I. According to Islamic teaching, "infidel" Great Britain's removal of Islamic rule from a land that, in Muslim eyes, belonged irrevocably to Allah should not be allowed to continue indefinitely.

When Great Britain withdrew, the new, independent State of Israel was born in that land in 1948 by decree of the General Assembly of the United Nations. Muslim nations saw that event as their opportunity to subjugate the land to Islamic rule once again. But, to do so, they would have to eliminate the fledgling Jewish state before it could become permanently entrenched. Almost immediately five Muslim nations jointly attacked Israel with massive forces. But, amazingly, against overwhelming odds, Israel won its War of Independence in 1949. Since then, Muslim nations made many more attempts to eradicate Israel. But each has failed.

Many Muslims worldwide regard the continued existence of the "infidel" State of Israel as a cancer that must be removed from an area of the world they believe should be exclusively Muslim. Thus, early in the 21st century, some Muslim nations and terrorist groups publicly declared their determination to accomplish what past attempts failed to do: completely eliminate Israel from the Middle East. Their plans, preparations, and actions overwhelmingly indicate that their determination is sincere.

Thus ownership of the land is the key issue that drives and motivates the conflict concerning Israel's existence in the Middle East. Who is the rightful owner of the land where the State of Israel exists? The answer is found in the Bible's revelation concerning the Abrahamic Covenant.

To understand the significance of that covenant, we must examine several aspects of that biblical revelation.

The Parties of the Abrahamic Covenant

A covenant is a binding commitment between at least two parties. It is impossible to have a one-party covenant. Even if one party makes all the commitment, that commitment is made to at least a second party.

Clearly, the first party of the Abrahamic Covenant is God. The other parties are Abraham, Isaac, Jacob, and their biological descendants: the Jewish people.

Genesis 15:18 records God's establishment of the covenant with Abraham:

> *On the same day the LORD made a covenant with Abram saying: "To your descendants I have given this land, from the river of Egypt to the great river, the River Euphrates—the Kenites, the Kenezzites, the Kadmonites, the Hittites, the Perizzites, the Rephaim, the Amorites, the Canaanites, the Girgashites, and the Jebusites."*

Because Abraham was the original party with whom God established the covenant, for centuries it has been designated the Abrahamic Covenant.

Some historical background is necessary to understand the next party of the covenant. For many years, Abraham's wife, Sarah, was incapable of bearing children. So Sarah asked Abraham to father children through her Egyptian maidservant, Hagar. Abraham granted Sarah's request and fathered a son through Hagar. That son was named Ishmael (16:1–4, 11).

Years later Abraham said to God, "Oh, that Ishmael might live before You!" (17:18). In essence, he was asking God to bless his son, Ishmael, by making him a party of the covenant God had already established with Abraham. However, God responded as follows:

> *No, Sarah your wife shall bear you a son, and you shall call his name Isaac; I will establish My covenant with him for an everlasting covenant, and with his descendants after him. And as for Ishmael, I have heard you. Behold, I have blessed him, and will make him fruitful, and will multiply him exceedingly. He shall beget twelve princes, and I will make him a great nation. But My covenant I will establish with Isaac, whom Sarah shall bear to you at this set time next year* (vv. 19–21).

God drew a distinction between Abraham's two sons and their biological descendants. This distinction is significant because it relates to the issue of who rightfully owns the land where the modern State of Israel is located. God said He would establish the Abrahamic Covenant with Isaac and his descendants, but He would not establish it with Ishmael or Ishmael's descendants.

Ishmael's descendants, the Ishmaelites, "dwelt in a twelvefold division in settlements and in movable camps in the desert of N Arabia, in the region between Havilah, Egypt, and the Euphrates."[1] In addition, "The Muslim Arabs, following Muhammad's example, claim descent from Ishmael."[2] Muslims also claim that Ishmael "and his mother Hagar were buried in the Ka'aba at Mecca."[3] To Muslims, the Ka'aba is the most sacred place of worship, and Mecca is the most sacred city on earth. Both the Ka'aba and Mecca are located in what today is Saudi Arabia.

The Ishmaelites are the Arab people. In light of this fact, God's statement that He would not establish the Abrahamic Covenant with Ishmael indicates that He did not establish it with the Arab people. God designated Isaac and his descendents—the Jewish people—to be the parties of the Abrahamic Covenant, and He refused to include Ishmael and the Arab people.

God did, however, promise to bless Ishmael and his descendants. Has God blessed the Arab people? Indeed He has. Arabs own and occupy more than 99.9 percent of the land across northern Africa and the Middle East. By contrast, the State of Israel owns and occupies less than one tenth of one percent of that land area. In addition, Arab people possess some of the largest oil reserves in the world, giving them access to great wealth and international influence.

After Isaac, God designated Jacob and his descendants as parties of the covenant. God told Jacob, "I am the LORD God of Abraham your father and the God of Isaac; the land on which you lie I will give to you and your descendants . . . and in you and in your seed all the families of the earth shall be blessed" (Gen. 28:13–14). In this statement God presented two promises of the Abrahamic Covenant: one regarding land and the other regarding blessing. God said He was establishing with Jacob and his descendants the covenant He had established earlier with Jacob's father, Isaac, and his grandfather Abraham.

Jacob fathered 12 sons who became the heads of the 12 tribes of the nation Israel. Thus Jacob and his descendants, the people of the nation of Israel, were made parties of the covenant.

So, God, Abraham, Isaac, Jacob, and the people of Israel are the sole parties of the Abrahamic Covenant. The next subject to examine in the issue of who rightfully owns the land is the national promises of that covenant.

The National Promises of the Abrahamic Covenant

God gave three national promises that relate exclusively to the nation of Israel.

The First Promise. God promised Abraham, "I will make you a great nation" (Gen. 12:2).

Later divine revelation signified that nation would consist of Abraham's biological descendants, the people of Israel. Later revelation also indicated the nation of Israel would be "great," not necessarily in size, but in significance. It would play key roles in fulfilling God's plan and purpose for mankind and history.

The Second Promise. God promised to give the land of Canaan, from the river of Egypt in the south to the Euphrates River in the north, to Abraham's biological descendants—the people of Israel—as an everlasting possession.

When Abraham entered Canaan, "the LORD appeared to" him "and said, 'To your descendants I will give this land'" (vv. 6–7). Later God told Abraham, "Lift your eyes now and look from the place where you are—northward, southward, eastward, and westward; for all the land which you see I give to you and your descendants forever" (13:14–15).

Genesis 15:18 records that God established the covenant with Abraham: "On the same day the LORD made a covenant with Abram, saying: 'To your descendants I have given this land, from the river of Egypt to the great river, the River Euphrates.'" The river of Egypt, the southern boundary of the land that God gave to Abraham's descendants, is the Wadi el-Arish, the southern boundary of the tribe of Judah (Josh. 15:1–4), not the Nile River.[4] The northern boundary, the Euphrates River, extends above Syria and Lebanon.

It is important to note that the descendants of Abraham to whom God refers in this promise of land ownership are Abraham's biological descendants—the literal people of Israel—not spiritual descendants. This fact is born out by the immediate context of the land promise. God said to Abraham,

> *Know certainly that your descendants will be strangers in a land that is not theirs, and will serve them, and they will afflict them four hundred years. And also the nation whom they will serve I will judge; afterward they will come out with great possessions* (Gen. 15:13–14).

God foretold (1) the migration of Jacob and his descendants to Egypt, (2) their later enslavement there, (3) God's judgment of Egypt with 10 supernatural plagues, and (4) Israel's Exodus from Egypt with Egyptian wealth under the leadership of Moses (Gen. 46—Ex. 14).

Later still, God stated to Abraham, "I give to you and your descendants after you the land in which you are a stranger, all the land of Canaan, as an everlasting possession; and I will be their God" (Gen. 17:8).

God confirmed the Abrahamic Covenant, including the land promise, to Isaac and his biological descendants, the people of Israel:

> *Then the LORD appeared to him and said: "Do not go down to Egypt; live in the land of which I shall tell you. Dwell in this land, and I will be with you and bless you; for to you and your descendants I give all these lands, and I will perform the oath which I swore to Abraham your father. And I will make your descendants multiply as the stars of heaven; I will give to your descendants all these lands; and in your seed all the nations of the earth shall be blessed"* (26:2–4).

God then confirmed the Abrahamic Covenant, including the land promise, to Jacob and his biological descendants, as we already have seen (28:13–14).

While the biological descendants of Abraham, Isaac, and Jacob were in bondage in Egypt, God made it exceedingly clear that they—literal, national Israel, not a surrogate, spiritual Israel—were the people He had covenanted to inherit the land:

> *God spoke to Moses and said to him: "I am the LORD. I appeared to Abraham, to Isaac, and to Jacob, . . . I have also established My covenant with them, to give them the land of Canaan, the land of their pilgrimage, in which they were strangers. And I have also heard the groaning of the children of Israel whom the Egyptians keep in bondage, and I have remembered My covenant. Therefore say to the children of Israel: 'I am the LORD; I will bring you out from under the burdens of the Egyptians, I will rescue you from their bondage, and I will redeem you with an outstretched arm and with great judgments. I will take you as My people, and I will be your God. Then you shall know that I am the LORD your God who brings you out from under the burdens of the Egyptians. And I will bring you into the land which I swore to give to Abraham, Isaac, and Jacob; and I will give it to you as a heritage: I am the LORD'"* (Ex. 6:2–8).

Many passages indicate that the people of Israel took ownership-possession of the Promised Land beginning with the generation that invaded and conquered it under the leadership of Joshua (Ex. 12:21–25; 13:5, 11; 33:1–2; Lev. 14:33–34; 20:24; 23:9–10; 25:1–2, 38; Num. 33:50–53; Dt. 1:8; 4:37–38; 6:10, 22–23; 10:11; 12:10; 19:1; 25:19; 26:1, 8–9, 15; 31:23; 32:49; 34:4; Josh. 1:1–6, 11; 21:43).

Deuteronomy 9:4–6 emphasizes that God did not covenant the people of Israel to inherit the land of Canaan because they were spiritually righteous. They were told,

Do not think in your heart, after the LORD your God has cast them out before you, saying, "Because of my righteousness the LORD has brought me in to possess this land"; but it is because of the wickedness of these nations that the LORD is driving them out from before you. It is not because of your righteousness or the uprightness of your heart that you go in to possess their land, but because of the wickedness of these nations that the LORD your God drives them out from before you, and that He may fulfill the word which the LORD swore to your fathers, to Abraham, Isaac, and Jacob. Therefore understand that the LORD your God is not giving you this good land to possess because of your righteousness, for you are a stiff-necked people.

Moses indicated that God had sworn to Abraham, Isaac, and Jacob that He would give to their biological descendants ownership of all the land of Canaan "forever" (Ex. 32:13).

The Third Promise. God promised to give the Abrahamic Covenant to Abraham's biological descendants, the people of Israel, for an everlasting covenant.

God told Abraham, "I will establish My covenant between Me and you and your descendants after you in their generations, for an everlasting covenant, to be God to you and your descendants after you" (Gen. 17:7). Later He told Abraham, "Sarah your wife shall bear you a son, and you shall call his name Isaac; I will establish my covenant with him for an everlasting covenant, and with his descendants after him" (v. 19).

In a psalm of thanksgiving that King David wrote, he made the following statements concerning God:

He remembers His covenant forever, the word which He commanded, for a thousand generations, the covenant which He made with Abraham, and His oath to Isaac, and confirmed it to Jacob for a statute, to Israel as an everlasting covenant, saying, "To you I will give the land of Canaan as the allotment of your inheritance," when they were few in number, indeed very few, and strangers in it (Ps. 105:8–12; cf. 1 Chr. 16:15–19).

So here are the facts: (1) God gave the land as an everlasting possession, meaning ownership was to be forever; (2) this land promise is part of the Abrahamic Covenant; (3) the covenant is everlasting; and (4) God established the Abrahamic Covenant exclusively with Abraham, Isaac, Jacob, and the people of Israel—not with Ishmael, the Arab people, or anyone else. Thus the Bible teaches without a doubt that Israel is the rightful owner of that land forever.

But is it possible that Israel could jeopardize the everlasting ownership of the land and everlasting nature of the Abrahamic Covenant through serious, persistent rebellion against God? Could not Israel break the covenant through such rebellion? To find the answer to these questions, we must examine the nature of the Abrahamic Covenant.

The Unconditional Nature of the Abrahamic Covenant

What do we mean when we say the covenant is unconditional? Simply this: the Abrahamic Covenant does not require Israel to meet any conditions in order for it to remain in effect and its promises to be fulfilled.

Evidences of the Covenant's Unconditional Nature. There are at least four lines of evidence of the unconditional nature of the Abrahamic Covenant.

First, who made all the promises in the covenant? God did. He made all the commitments. Abraham made none. Isaac made none. Jacob made none. And the people of Israel made none.

Scripture emphasizes this distinction in several ways. It asserts that it was God who made or established the Abrahamic Covenant (Gen. 15:18; 17:7, 19, 21; 1 Chr. 16:16–18; Ps. 105:9–10). It refers to the Abrahamic Covenant as "His covenant" (Ex. 2:24; 1 Chr.

16:15; Ps. 105:8; Lk. 1:72–73), and it records God calling it "My covenant" (Gen. 17:2, 4, 7, 19, 21; Ex. 6:4–5; Lev. 26:42, 44; Jud. 2:1).

This means, then, that the covenant remaining in effect and its promises being fulfilled are dependent totally and exclusively on God being faithful to His Word. The only way the covenant could be rendered inoperative and its promises void is if God were to break His Word. But God said to the nation of Israel, "I led you up from Egypt and brought you to the land of which I swore to your fathers; and I said, 'I will never break My covenant with you'" (Jud. 2:1; cf. Ex. 32:13). God further declared that, in spite of Israel's rebellion against Him, "when they are in the land of their enemies, I will not cast them away, nor shall I abhor them, to utterly destroy them and break My covenant with them; for I am the LORD their God" (Lev. 26:44).

Second, the way in which God formally established the covenant with Abraham testifies strongly to its unconditional nature. After God had promised more than once to give the land to Abraham and his descendants, He promised it again. In Genesis 15:7 God said to Abraham, "I am the LORD, who brought you out of Ur of the Chaldeans, to give you this land to inherit it."

Abraham responded, "Lord GOD, how shall I know that I will inherit it?" (v. 8). In essence Abraham was saying, "Lord, you keep promising to give the land to me, but how can I be certain that you will do it? Do something concrete that will confirm to me that you will do it."

God granted Abraham's request by instructing him to do something that seems strange to most people in the modern world. He told Abraham to cut several large animals in half and to arrange the halves side by side with a path between the halves (vv. 9–10). Later, "when the sun was going down, a deep sleep fell upon Abram" (v. 12). That deep sleep rendered Abraham inactive.

Then, when the sun went down and it was dark, there appeared a smoking oven with a burning torch that moved between the pieces of the animals (v. 17). The fire of the burning torch is the same fire that appeared later to Moses at the burning bush (Ex. 3:2–3). It appeared as a pillar of fire enshrouded in a cloud during the Israelites' Exodus journey from Egypt (Ex. 13:21–22; 14:24) and during their wilderness wandering (Ex. 16:10; Neh. 9:19). It came to the top of Mount Sinai when God met with Moses to give the Law to Israel (Ex. 19:9, 16–18; 24:12, 15–18). It came to the Tabernacle (Ex. 40:34–38) and Israel's first Temple (2 Chr. 7:1–3) when they were dedicated as God's worship structures. It remained continuously with the nation of Israel for several centuries.

Every time this special fire appeared, it signified that God was present in a unique sense. At the burning bush it meant God was present to appoint Moses to be His deliverer of Israel from its slavery in Egypt. During Israel's Exodus from Egypt and wilderness journey, it demonstrated God was with the Israelites to guide, protect, and provide for them. When it descended to Mount Sinai, it indicated that God had come there to enter into another covenant relationship with Israel. Its descent to the Tabernacle and Temple revealed that God was coming to dwell in a unique sense in those structures.

Because this fire remained with Israel for several centuries and signified God's unique presence, through time it became known as the Shekinah Glory of God. The term *Shekinah* is derived from a word that means "to dwell."[5]

Since the fire of the burning torch that appeared while Abraham was in a deep sleep was the same fire as the Shekinah Glory of God, God was present in a unique sense. When it appeared, it passed between the halves of the animals that Abraham had cut earlier. Thus the unique presence of God passed between the cut animals.

Why would God move between the halves of the animals? In the ancient Middle East a significant way to establish a covenant was as follows: animals would be cut in half, and the halves would be arranged side by side with a path between. If all the parties of a covenant were making commitments, all of them would pass between the halves of the animals. (See Jeremiah 34:8–10, 18–19).

If only one party was making commitments, that party alone would pass between the halves.

What was the significance of establishing a covenant in this manner? In essence, by passing between the halves of the cut animals, the parties were saying, "May the same thing be done to me as has been done to these animals if I don't keep my commitments in this covenant."

God alone passed between the halves of the animals when He established the Abrahamic Covenant. Abraham did not and could not pass between them because he was in a deep sleep. For that reason the Scriptures say, "On the same day the LORD made a covenant with Abram" (Gen. 15:18). It does not say the Lord and Abram made a covenant.

Abraham made no commitments. God made them all. Therefore, Abraham was not required to meet any conditions for the covenant to remain in effect and its promises to be fulfilled. Since God made all the commitments, the covenant remaining in effect and its promises being fulfilled depend exclusively on God being faithful to His Word.

Third, another evidence of the Abrahamic Covenant being unconditional in relationship to Israel comes from King David. Even after the nation had sinned in numerous ways over many centuries, David regarded the Abrahamic Covenant to be in effect in his time. In 1 Chronicles 16:15–18 he wrote the following comments to Israel: "Remember His covenant forever, the word which He commanded, for a thousand generations, the covenant which He made with Abraham, and His oath to Isaac, and confirmed it to Jacob for a statute, to Israel for an everlasting covenant, saying, 'To you I will give the land of Canaan as the allotment of your inheritance.'" David's comments indicated that Israel's numerous sins against God for centuries up to David's time did not jeopardize the everlasting ownership of the land or everlasting nature of the Abrahamic Covenant.

Fourth, if there were a sin capable of repealing or ending Israel's everlasting ownership of the land and the everlasting nature of the

Abrahamic Covenant, surely it would have been Israel's rejection of God's Son, Jesus Christ, as the Messiah and Savior when He was present in the nation. But even after most of the people of that generation of Israel spurned Jesus, the apostle Peter still regarded them as being related to the Abrahamic Covenant.

One day when the apostles Peter and John were entering Israel's Temple in Jerusalem, God enabled Peter to heal a man who was born lame. The healed man walked, leaped, and praised God as he entered the Temple with the apostles. This miraculous healing drew a huge crowd (Acts 3:1–11). When Peter saw the crowd, he said to the people,

> *Men of Israel, why do you marvel at this? Or why look so intently at us, as though by our own power or godliness we had made this man walk? The God of Abraham, Isaac, and Jacob, the God of our fathers, glorified His Servant Jesus, whom you delivered up and denied in the presence of Pilate, when he was determined to let Him go. But you denied the Holy One and the Just, and asked for a murderer to be granted to you, and killed the Prince of life, whom God raised from the dead, of which we are witnesses* (vv. 12–15).

Apparently this crowd either consisted of, or at least contained, people who cried out for Jesus' crucifixion when He was on trial before Pilate.

Despite this great sin of which these people were guilty, Peter went on to say to them, "You are sons of the prophets, and of the covenant which God made with our fathers, saying to Abraham, 'And in your seed all the families of the earth shall be blessed'" (v. 25). This statement to Abraham was one of God's promises in the Abrahamic Covenant (Gen. 12:3; 18:17–18; 22:15–18; 26:1–4; 28:10, 13–14). Therefore, Peter was referring to the Abrahamic Covenant.

In fact, Peter said "You are" (present tense), not "You were" (past tense), "sons of the" Abrahamic Covenant. That Peter used the present tense indicates he still regarded these guilty people as being related to the Abrahamic Covenant. In other words, their sin did not repeal or terminate Israel's everlasting ownership of the land or the everlasting nature of the Abrahamic Covenant. They continued to be in that covenant relationship with God.

The only way a covenant could be broken was if a party of the covenant later broke the promises or commitments he made in establishing the covenant. If he made no promises or commitments, there were no parts of the covenant that were binding on him or that he was obligated or responsible to keep. Since Abraham, Isaac, Jacob, and the people of Israel made no promises or commitments in the establishment of the Abrahamic Covenant, there were no parts of that covenant that were binding on them or that they were obligated or responsible to keep. Thus there is no way the Jewish people could break that particular covenant.

Effects of the Abrahamic Covenant on Israel

The Covenant Guarantees Israel's Permanent Existence as a Nation. Since there is no way Israel could break the Abrahamic Covenant, and God declared that He will never break it and that the covenant is everlasting, then the people of Israel must exist forever. The only way they could be eliminated would be if the Abrahamic Covenant were not everlasting.

Several biblical passages indicate that, despite Israel's unbelief and rebellion against God, the Jewish nation never will be destroyed. For example, although the Israelites sinned by rejecting God as their King in favor of a human king, Samuel assured them, "the LORD will not forsake His people, for His great name's sake, because it has pleased the LORD to make you His people" (1 Sam. 12:12, 17, 22).

Even when the people of Israel were so incurably wicked that God was bringing the Babylonians to the nation to destroy Jerusalem and the Temple, He declared, "'I am with you,' says the LORD, 'to save you; though I make a full end of all nations where I have scattered you, yet I will not make a complete end of you.

But I will correct you in justice, and will not let you go altogether unpunished"' (Jer. 30:11).

In Romans 11:28–29 the apostle Paul indicated that, even *while* the people of Israel *are* enemies of the gospel, as touching God's election of them to be in a *permanent* unique relationship with Him as a nation (Dt. 7:6; 2 Sam. 7:23–24), they "*are* beloved for the sake of the fathers" (Dt. 4:37; 7:8, emphasis added), "for the gifts and the calling of God are irrevocable."

G. Schrenk stated that, in Romans 11:28, Paul used the term *the election* for "the election of all Israel in the fathers," and "Here the reference is not to a part but to the whole people."[6]

William Arndt and Wilbur Gingrich said the term translated "gifts" "refers to the privileges granted to the people of Israel,"[7] and Hans Conzelmann indicated that these gifts to Israel "are more precisely listed in Romans 9:4f."[8] According to Romans 9:4, that list includes "the covenants" and "the promises" that God gave to the Israelites, Paul's "countrymen according to the flesh" (v. 3).

Arndt and Gingrich signified that the term translated "irrevocable" is used of something one does not take back."[9] O. Michel asserted that this "is a reference to God's faithfulness and to the reliability of His promise."[10]

Thus, in Romans 11:28–29, Paul indicated that unsaved Jewish people today are still in the Abrahamic Covenant relationship with God, together with its national promises, in spite of their rejection of and opposition to the gospel concerning Jesus Christ. This is so not because they deserve this continued relationship (no human beings, Jewish or Gentile, deserve it), but because God irrevocably committed Himself to a covenant relationship that is everlasting with the entire nation of Israel. And God is faithful to His commitments.

The Abrahamic Covenant's guarantee of Israel's permanent existence as a nation has two significant implications. First, this guarantee explains the reason for the Jewish people's continued existence despite repeated persecutions and attempts to exterminate them.

Second, this guarantee stands as an unyielding, immovable stone against which anti-Semitism will dash itself to bits in the future Tribulation when it makes its last and greatest effort to destroy Israel. No matter how ugly and powerful anti-Semitism may become, it will never be able to annihilate the Jewish people.

The Covenant Guarantees Israel Permanent Ownership of the Promised Land. Because (1) the Abrahamic Covenant is unconditional in nature, (2) God promised to give the land of Canaan to Abraham and the people of Israel forever as an everlasting possession, and (3) the Israelites took ownership-possession of the Promised Land under the leadership of Joshua, then Israel must retain ownership of that land today and throughout the future.

Furthermore, Israel did not have to live in the land continuously in order to maintain ownership. Occupancy and ownership are not the same thing. Some landlords own many properties, but they do not live in all of them. Ownership does not require personal occupancy by the owner. Thus Israel's dispersions from its land because of sin have not ended its ownership of the land. Because of God's irrevocable commitment to give permanent ownership of the land to Israel as an everlasting possession, from God's perspective Israel is the rightful owner of the land now and forever.

Because this is so, God has promised that, in the future, He will regather to their own land the Jewish people who are still scattered among the nations; and He will plant them there forever (Ezek. 37:21–28; Amos 9:14–15).

Application

The biblical revelation concerning the nation of Israel and the Abrahamic Covenant prompts three main areas of application for Christians.

First, because of God's irrevocable commitment to give ownership of the land to Israel forever, Christians should support both Israel's right to exist as a nation-state in that land without being terrorized and to defend itself against its enemies. And Christians should pray for the peace of Jerusalem and the nation of Israel.

Second, because the majority of the Jewish people in the land are there in unbelief, Christians must recognize there is no guarantee that Israel always does what is right. Are Christians always right in what they do?

Third, Christians are not to hate the Arab people. God sent His Son to provide salvation as much for them as for the people of Israel and all other people. In addition, though God did not establish the Abrahamic Covenant with the Arabs, He promised to bless them. And God has blessed them greatly with a large population, ownership of massive land areas in northern Africa and the Middle East, and huge oil reserves.

Non-Arab Christians must be sensitive to the fact that a good number of Middle East Arabs have genuinely trusted Jesus Christ as Savior. Many of them are persecuted for their faith, even to the extent of imprisonment, torture, rape, threat of death, and actual death. We should pray for these brothers and sisters in Christ and for the salvation of many more Arabs.

ENDNOTES

[1] Fred E. Young, "Ishmaelites," *Wycliffe Bible Encyclopedia*, ed. Charles F. Pfeiffer, Howard F. Vos, and John Rea (Chicago: Moody Press, 1975), 1:862.

[2] Ibid.

[3] Ibid., 861.

[4] Clyde E. Harrington, "Egypt, River of," *The New International Dictionary of the Bible, Pictorial Edition*, ed. J. D. Douglas, Merrill C. Tenney (Grand Rapids: Zondervan, 1987), 298.

[5] J. Barton Payne, *The Theology of the Older Testament* (Grand Rapids: Zondervan, 1962), 361.

[6] G. Schrenk, "ekloge," *Theological Dictionary of the New Testament* (hereafter cited as *TDNT*), ed. Gerhard Kittel, trans./ed. Geoffrey W. Bromiley, translated from *Theologisches Worterbuch zum Neuen Testament* (Grand Rapids: Eerdmans, 1967), 4:179.

[7] William F. Arndt and F. Wilbur Gingrich, eds./trans., "charisma," *A Greek-English Lexicon of the New Testament and Other Early Chrisitan Literature* (1952: translation and

adaptation of Walter Bauer's *Griechisch-Deutsches Worterbuch zu den Schriften des Neuen Testaments und der ubrigen urchristlichen Literatur,* 4th ed.; Chicago: University of Chicago Press, 1957), 887.

[8] Hans Conzelmann, "charisma," *TDNT,* ed. Gerhard Friedrich, trans./ed. Geoffrey W. Bromiley, translated from *Theologisches Worterbuch zum Neuen Testament* (Grand Rapids: Eerdmans, 1974), 9:403 n. 10.

[9] Arndt and Gingrich, "ametameletos," 44.

[10] O. Michel, "metamelomai," *TDNT,* ed. Gerhard Kittel, trans./ed. Geoffrey W. Bromiley, 4:629.

CHAPTER 4

ISRAEL AND JERUSALEM

In a *U.S. News & World Report* editorial, Editor-in-Chief Mortimer B. Zuckerman indicated in 2000 that the issue of who is going to control Jerusalem must be settled before peace can exist in the Middle East. "Were all the territorial issues to be resolved, except for Jerusalem," he wrote, "Jerusalem itself would become the focal point for a future conflict—and a Jerusalem-centered conflict will become a religious war between Jews and the Muslims."[1]

Mr. Zuckerman is correct. The issue of who will control Jerusalem is extremely explosive. On the one hand, Jerusalem is the Jewish people's most important and sacred city in the world. For many centuries it was Israel's capital city where the Jews went to worship God at the nation's first two Temples on the Temple Mount.

On the other hand, Jerusalem is the third most sacred Muslim city in the world. Only Mecca and Medina, in Arabia (today Saudi Arabia), where Islam began in the 600s A.D., are more sacred than Jerusalem. Muslims teach that Muhammad their prophet ascended to heaven one night to receive revelation from God and that he did so from Jerusalem. Thus they believe the city should be under Muslim control.

Muslims also believe that once they have ruled an area of the world, that area belongs irrevocably to Allah. If a non-Muslim force should succeed in removing Islamic rule from that area, that removal dishonors Allah. Thus, for the sake of Allah's honor, the non-Muslim force must be eliminated and Islamic rule restored. During the Middle Ages and later, Jerusalem was ruled several times by Muslims. But from 1917 to 1948 Jerusalem was ruled by

Great Britain; from 1948 to 1967 the western half of the city was ruled by Israel; and from 1967 to the present, the entire city has been ruled by Israel.

Since Muslims regard Great Britain and Israel as infidel nations, they believe that, for the sake of Allah's honor, they must restore Islamic rule to all of Jerusalem. If they are true to their faith, they cannot accept anything less.

Jerusalem's Significance to God

Without a doubt, Jerusalem has greater significance to God than any other city in the world.

God declared, "This is Jerusalem; I have set her in the midst of the nations and the countries all around her" (Ezek. 5:5). In other words, God is the One who determined where Jerusalem was to be located.

Jerusalem is the city where God chose "to put His name" (1 Ki. 14:21). He did not choose to put His name in any other city.

God desired and chose Jerusalem to be the city where He would dwell forever (Ps. 132:13–14). He never desired or chose to dwell in any other city forever.

God's Shekinah Glory dwelt in the Temple at Jerusalem (2 Chr. 7:1–3). So God was dwelling there in a unique sense at Jerusalem.

God called Jerusalem "My city" (Isa. 45:13). Notice the possessive pronoun *My*. He indicated that Jerusalem belonged uniquely to Him.

Jerusalem was called "the city of our God" (Ps. 48:1). This was the psalmist's way of acknowledging that Jerusalem belonged uniquely to God.

The Bible calls Jerusalem "the holy city" (Isa. 52:1; Mt. 4:5). The word translated "holy" means "divided." To be holy is to be divided from other persons and things—divided in the sense of being different, distinct, or unique. Thus, when the Bible calls Jerusalem "the holy city," it means God divided that city from all other cities of the world. He divided, or set it apart, to be different, distinct, or unique in contrast with all other cities.

God's Son, Jesus Christ, was crucified outside the ancient city of Jerusalem (Heb. 13:12).

God's Son was resurrected bodily from the dead outside Jerusalem (Jn. 19:41).

God's Son ascended to heaven from the Mount of Olives outside Jerusalem (Acts 1:4, 9, 12).

The church was born in the city of Jerusalem (Acts 2:1–5).

These biblical facts indicate that the city of Jerusalem has overwhelming significance to God. It is uniquely related to Him in ways that are not true of any other city in the world.

The History of Jerusalem

The Bible first mentions Jerusalem in Genesis 14:18 where it is called Salem. It was ruled by Melchizedek, a godly king and priest of God and a contemporary of Abraham.

For several centuries thereafter, it was a Jebusite city (Josh. 15:8; 18:28). Israel did not conquer Jerusalem from the Jebusites for several centuries after their invasion and conquest of the land of Canaan under Joshua (Josh. 15:63; Jud. 1:21; 19:10). Finally, around 998 B.C. David and his forces conquered Jerusalem from the Jebusites; and David made Jerusalem his headquarters and the capital of the united kingdom of Israel (1 Chr. 11:4–9). Later David purchased the threshing floor of Ornan the Jebusite as the place at Jerusalem to offer sacrifices to God (1 Chr. 21:18–28). Later that place became the Temple Mount (2 Chr. 3:1).

Because of Israel's persistent rebellion against God for approximately four centuries after David, God withdrew His protective presence, as signified by the withdrawal of His Shekinah Glory from the Temple and Jerusalem in the early 500s B.C. (Ezek. 9:3; 10:4, 18–19; 11:22–23). Without God's protective presence, the Babylonians were able to destroy Jerusalem and the first Temple in 586 B.C. (2 Chr. 36:11–21; Jer. 52:1–14). That destruction was a traumatic part of the 70-year Babylonian Captivity.

In 539 B.C. Medo-Persia conquered Babylon. Now the Jewish people were under Medo-Persian rule. The next year King Cyrus of Medo-Persia officially ended the Jewish captivity. Jews were permitted to return to their homeland to rebuild. Many did return. Under the leadership of Zerubbabel, Ezra, and Nehemiah, they built Jerusalem and the second Temple. (See the books of Ezra and Nehemiah.)

Before this building project was completed, God sent the angel Gabriel to Daniel to reveal that, after the Messiah would be cut off with a violent death, this new city of Jerusalem and the second Temple would be destroyed by a particular people (Dan. 9:21–26).

Jesus also foretold this future destruction. As He approached Jerusalem on the day of His triumphal entry, Jesus wept over the city, saying,

> *If you had known, even you, especially in this your day, the things that make for your peace! But now they are hidden from your eyes. For days will come upon you when your enemies will build an embankment around you, surround you and close you in on every side, and level you, and your children within you, to the ground; and they will not leave in you one stone upon another, because you did not know the time of your visitation* (Lk. 19:41–44).

On another occasion, when His disciples showed Him the buildings of the second Temple, Jesus said, "Do you not see all these things? Assuredly, I say to you, not one stone shall be left here upon another, that shall not be thrown down" (Mt. 24:1–2).

Several decades after Jesus was cut off with a violent death, His prophecies and those delivered to Daniel concerning the destruction of Jerusalem and the Temple were fulfilled. Roman legions surrounded Jerusalem in A.D. 67 and besieged it for three years. In A.D. 70 they broke through Jerusalem's defenses, killed many of the people inside, and leveled the city and Temple to the ground. That traumatic event ended Israel's rule of Jerusalem and its existence as a nation-state.

For the next 1,878 years (from A.D. 70 to 1948) Jerusalem was ruled by the following succession of Gentile powers: Romans (until A.D. 324), Byzantines (324–614), Persians (614–629), Byzantines (629–638), Arab Muslims (638–1099), Crusaders (1099–1187), Muslims (1187–1229), Crusaders and Muslims (1229–1244), Khwarizm Turks (1244–1250), Mamluks (1250–1516), Ottoman Turks (1516–1917), and Great Britain (1917–1948).[2] Throughout all this time Jewish people lived in the land, but not always in Jerusalem. It is significant to note that not one of these Gentile powers ever made Jerusalem the capital of its kingdom or empire. This means that Israel was the last nation to have Jerusalem as its capital.

On November 29, 1947, the UN General Assembly approved partitioning Palestine into two divisions. One was to be an Arab state; the other, a Jewish state. Jerusalem was to be under international rule. The Jewish people accepted this United Nations decision, but Arab nations rejected it and promised it would lead to war.

After November 29, 1947, turmoil, created by Arab attempts to prevent the new State of Israel from being established, prompted thousands of Arabs to leave for neighboring Arab nations. Once the Jews announced the establishment of the State of Israel on May 14, 1948, Arab nations urged more Arabs to leave Israel and come to their nations temporarily.[3] The Arab nations intended to attack the new State of Israel and drive it into the Mediterranean Sea.[4] Then the Arabs who left Israel could return and possess the entire land.

The Jews encouraged the Arabs to stay in Israel and maintain their homes, businesses, and way of life. Between 140,000 and 157,000 chose to remain in independent Israel.[5] They became full citizens of Israel with the same rights and privileges as Jewish citizens, including voting rights and election of Arab representatives to Israel's Knesset. Those who stayed prospered, and so have their descendants.

Estimates differ concerning how many Arabs left Israel for Arab nations in 1948. They vary between 430,000 and 650,000.

One study claimed the number of those who left in May 1948 was 539,000.[6]

Arab armies from Egypt, Jordan, Lebanon, Syria, and Iraq were joined by soldiers from Saudi Arabia in a multipronged attack against the fledgling Jewish state almost immediately after it announced its establishment as a nation.[7] In Cairo, Azzam Pasha, secretary-general of the Arab League, boasted, "This will be a war of extermination and a momentous massacre which will be spoken of like the Mongolian massacres and Crusades."[8]

Because the Arabs had many more soldiers and superior weapons, they were confident they would eliminate Israel from the Middle East. But contrary to what appeared would be the obvious result of the fighting, Israel won this War of Independence. As a result, it gained control of the western half of Jerusalem, the newer part of the city. Jordan continued to maintain control of the eastern half (the old part), including the Temple Mount.

Since this war against Israel had the opposite result of what the Arab nations had anticipated, they were now faced with a major problem. What was to be done with all the Arab people who had left Israel to enter the Arab nations before they attacked Israel? In spite of the fact that these nations had more than enough space and employment opportunities to absorb these displaced people, and even had need for more manpower, almost all of these nations refused to integrate them into their societies. Instead, they forced most of them to return to areas adjacent to the new State of Israel and become refugees in difficult living circumstances.[9]

Ralph Galloway, a former director of UNRWA (United Nations Relief and Works Agency), stated, "The Arab states do not want to solve the refugee problem. They want to keep it as an open sore, as an affront to the United Nations, and as a weapon against Israel." He accused Arab leaders of having no concern about "whether Arab refugees live or die."[10]

The Western news media has basically ignored the fact that another major refugee problem, a Jewish one, developed at the same time. Across North Africa and the Middle East, hundreds of thousands of Jews were forced to leave Arab nations where their families had lived for generations, some for as many as 2,000 years. They lost their homes and businesses. Research has indicated that the number of these Jewish refugees equaled that of the Arabs.[11] In contrast with the multitudes of displaced Arabs who were denied places to settle in the nations of their brother Arabs, hundreds of thousands of displaced Jews found permanent residence in the new State of Israel.[12]

From 1948 to 1967, a period of 19 years, Jerusalem remained divided between Israel (controlling the western half of the city) and Jordan (controlling the eastern half, including the Old City and Temple Mount).

On December 10, 1949, the UN General Assembly approved a resolution calling for international control of the entire city of Jerusalem. In other words, the city was to be removed from Israeli and Jordanian control. On December 13, Israel's government reacted to this resolution by proclaiming Jerusalem its eternal capital and announcing the transfer of its offices and the Knesset to Jerusalem.

Both Israel and Jordan opposed the United Nation's proposal to internationalize Jerusalem. As a result, the UN proposal remained on the record but was not put into effect.

Most nations refused to recognize Jerusalem as Israel's capital and set up their embassies and legates in Tel Aviv instead. Through time, however, that began to change. By 1972, 22 nations had set up embassies in Jerusalem, and 11 other nations had consulates or consulates-general in that city.

By early June 1967, three Arab nations—Egypt, Jordan, and Syria—had moved large military forces to Israel's borders. On June 5, the Six-Day War began. On June 7, Israel captured from Jordan the eastern half of Jerusalem, including the Old City and Temple Mount. Now, for the first time since A.D. 70, Israel ruled all of Jerusalem. But, in spite of this, the Israeli government granted complete authority over the Temple Mount to Muslim religious leaders in Israel. That policy has continued ever since.

Thus Muslims determine who may or may not go up on the Temple Mount.

Strong Statements Concerning Jerusalem

As the years have progressed, the Muslims have only grown stronger and more militant in their determination to exterminate Israel and take control of Jerusalem.

On May 9, 1997, the Palestinian Authority's mufti of Jerusalem, Sheikh Ekrima Sabri, declared the following over Voice of Palestine Radio: "Despite all the conspiracies, Jerusalem and Palestine from the [Jordan] River to the [Mediterranean] Sea will remain Islamic until judgment day."[13]

On July 11, 1997, Voice of Palestine Radio broadcast Sheikh Sabri's weekly sermon from the al-Aqsa mosque located on Jerusalem's Temple Mount. The following are excerpts:

> *Oh Allah, destroy America, for she is ruled by Zionist Jews. . . . Allah will paint the White House black!... The Muslims say to Britain, to France and to all the infidel nations that Jerusalem is Arab. We shall not respect anyone else's wishes regarding her. The only relevant party is the Islamic nation, which will not allow infidel nations to interfere. . . . Allah shall take revenge on behalf of his prophet against the colonialist settlers who are sons of monkeys and pigs. . . . Forgive us, Muhammad, for the acts of these sons of monkeys and pigs, who sought to harm your sanctity.*[14]

By contrast, Benjamin Netanyahu, a former prime minister of Israel who was reelected in 2009, made this statement: "Jerusalem is Israel's capital, will never be divided, and will remain the capital of the State of Israel, the capital of the Jewish people, for ever and ever."[15]

While Netanyahu was prime minister in the 1990s, Ariel Sharon headed the Likud Party. Sharon wrote the following:

> *The denial, the refusal to recognize Israel's sovereignty over Jerusalem, has been going on for over half a century. In UN*

General Assembly Resolution No. 181 of November 1947, it was proposed that the city of Jerusalem be internationalized. The Arab nations rejected the resolution and promptly launched a war against the small Jewish community in the Land of Israel. Our people made a heroic stand against the onslaught of seven Arab armies that invaded Israel. Thousands of our young people died in this struggle, and tens of thousands were wounded. But we won. . . . That UN resolution, therefore, calling for the internationalization of Jerusalem is null and void; it no longer exists. . . . Jerusalem has always been the national capital of the Jewish people, and of no other. . . . At this critical juncture of the struggle for the maintenance of full Israeli sovereignty over Jerusalem, the national interest requires that - as is evident also in the practice of other countries - the realization of Israel's sovereignty must, and indeed always will, take precedence over recognition by external bodies. . . . we must make the following absolutely clear, here and now, to the Palestinians as well as to friends and rivals alike, in Europe and throughout the world. . . . Full Israeli sovereignty over Jerusalem, the united and eternal capital of the Jewish people, is not and will never be a subject for negotiation with any foreign entity. The Netanyahu government will continue to insist on this, and I am confident that with will and determination, our effort will be successful"[16]

There could not be more diametrically opposed statements than these concerning who has the right to control Jerusalem.

A Biblical Perspective

The issue of Jerusalem has the potential to explode catastrophically in the face of the whole world. Consequently, world leaders have no choice but to deal with it.

Many may conclude there can be no lasting peace in the Middle East unless control of Jerusalem is taken away from Israel and placed in international hands, as the United Nations has resolved twice in the past. If Israel resists such action, the entire world may come against it with great force in an attempt to bring peace.

The Bible presents a prophetic perspective of what will happen when the nations of the world bother themselves with Jerusalem. Several biblical passages reveal that the leaders and armies of all nations will come against Israel and Jerusalem by the end of the future Tribulation (Joel 3:9–15; Zeph. 3:8; Zech. 12—14; Rev. 16:12–16; 19:19).

As these forces wage war against Israel, two-thirds of the Jewish people in the land will perish. Zechariah 13:8 states, "'And it shall come to pass in all the land,' says the LORD, 'that two-thirds in it shall be cut off and die, but one-third shall be left in it.'"

God will use this war against Israel to draw the remaining one-third to Him and His Messiah: "I will bring the one-third through the fire, will refine them as silver is refined, and test them as gold is tested. They will call on My name, and I will answer them. I will say, 'This is My people'; and each one will say, 'The LORD is My God'" (Zech. 13:9).

Once the remnant repents of its rebellion against God and the Messiah, God will destroy the leaders and armies of all the nations of the world when they have Jerusalem surrounded:

> *"For there I will sit to judge all the surrounding nations." The LORD also will roar from Zion, and utter His voice from Jerusalem; the heavens and earth will shake; but the LORD will be a shelter for His people, and the strength of the children of Israel. "So you shall know that I am the LORD your God, dwelling in Zion My holy mountain. Then Jerusalem shall be holy, and no aliens shall ever pass through her again"* (Joel 3:12, 16–17).

In Zephaniah 3:8 God said, "My determination is to gather the nations to My assembly of kingdoms, to pour on them My indignation, all My fierce anger."

God said this concerning the future:

Behold, I will make Jerusalem a cup of drunkenness to all the surrounding peoples, when they lay siege against Judah and Jerusalem. And it shall happen in that day that I will make Jerusalem a very heavy stone for all peoples; all who would heave it away will surely be cut in pieces, though all nations of the earth are gathered against it. . . . In that day the LORD will defend the inhabitants of Jerusalem; . . . It shall be in that day that I will seek to destroy all the nations that come against Jerusalem (Zech. 12:2–3, 8–9).

I will gather all the nations to battle against Jerusalem; . . . But the remnant of the people shall not be cut off from the city. Then the LORD will go forth and fight against those nations, as He fights in the day of battle. And in that day His feet will stand on the Mount of Olives, which faces Jerusalem on the east. . . . And this shall be the plague with which the LORD will strike all the people who fought against Jerusalem: Their flesh shall dissolve while they stand on their feet, their eyes shall dissolve in their sockets, and their tongues shall dissolve in their mouths (14:2–4, 12).

Revelation 16:14 foretells that, when the sixth bowl judgment will be administered near the end of the Tribulation, "the kings of the earth and of the whole world" will be gathered "to the battle of that great day of God Almighty." Revelation 19:11–21 promises that, when Jesus Christ will come from heaven to judge and wage war after the Tribulation, He will kill "the kings of the earth, and their armies" that have gathered to destroy Israel (v. 19).

Through these prophetic passages God revealed that He will faithfully prevent Israel from being annihilated, will bring it into right relationship with Himself and the Messiah, and will permanently establish Jerusalem as the capital city of that nation.

ENDNOTES

[1] Mortimer B. Zuckerman, "Using hate against Israel," *U.S. News & World Report* 128, no. 23 (2000), 72.

[2] *Jerusalem*, in *Israel Pocket Library* (Jerusalem: Keter Publishing, 1973), 38–167.

[3] Joan Peters, *From Time Immemorial* (Chicago: J.KAP Publishing, 1984), 12–13.

[4] Ibid.

[5] Ibid., 16 n.

[6] Ibid.,16.

[7] "The War of Independence: 1947–49," *Facts About Israel* (Jerusalem: Division of Information, Ministry for Foreign Affairs, 1973), 42–44.

[8] Ibid., 42.

[9] Peters, 19–25.

[10] Terence Prittie, "Middle East Refugees," in Michael Curtis et al., eds., *The Palestinians: People, History, Politics* (New Brunswick, NJ: Transaction Books, 1975), 71.

[11] Peters, 25.

[12] Irving Howe and Carl Gershman, eds., *Israel, the Arabs, and the Middle East* (New York: Bantam, 1972), 168.

[13] Ekrima Sabri, "Quotes to Note," *Middle East Digest* 8, no. 7 (July 1997) <http://cdn-friends-icej.ca/medigest/fmed0797.html>.

[14] Ekrima Sabri, Independent Media Review & Analysis, "Senior PA Official: 'Destroy America'—'Jews: Sons of Monkeys & Pigs,'" trans. Dr. Aaron Lerner, July 13, 1997 <freeman.org/m_online/aug97/lerner1.htm>.

[15] "Benjamin Netanyahu Quotes" <brainyquote.com/quotes/quotes/b/benjaminne164736.html>.

[16] Ariel Sharon, "Still fighting for Jerusalem" March 19, 1999 <mfa.gov.il/MFA/Foreign%20Relations/Israels%20Foreign%20Relations%20since%201947/1998-1999/153%20Still%20Fighting%20for%20Jerusalem-%20an%20article%20in%20th>.

CHAPTER 5

ISRAEL, ISLAM,
AND THE ANTICHRIST

During the Middle Ages and later, the land the nation of Israel had owned and inhabited for many centuries was subjugated several times by Muslim forces. The last of those forces was the Turkish Ottoman Empire that ruled the land for some 400 years. Great Britain ended Islamic rule with its defeat of Turkey during World War I and itself ruled the land until 1948 when the new, independent State of Israel was established there as mandated by the United Nations.

Since 1948 several Muslim nations have attempted to eliminate Israel. Despite their failures, some Muslim nations, such as Syria and Iran, together with Muslim terrorist organizations, persist in pursuing the Islamic goal of the annihilation of Israel. This continued pursuit is significant in light of what the Scriptures reveal concerning the future of Israel and Islam.

In the Future

Israel vs. Egypt and Syria. The prophet Daniel recorded the following revelation from God: "At the time of the end the king of the South shall attack him; and the king of the North shall come against him like a whirlwind, with chariots, horsemen, and with many ships" (Dan. 11:40).

Several questions must be asked concerning this prophecy. First, what is meant by "the time of the end"? Jews in biblical times divided all of history since the fall of man into two ages.

The first was the age before the Messiah comes to rule the world in the future political Kingdom of God. To their way of thinking, that would be the present age of history. The second was when Messiah would be present ruling the world, which they called "the age to come" or "the Messianic age."[1]

Therefore, the context of Daniel 11:40 prompts the conclusion that "the time of the end" in that verse refers to the end-times period of the present age *before* Messiah comes to rule the world in the future Kingdom of God. Other prophetic passages reveal the end-times period of the present age will be characterized by tribulation, including an unparalleled time of trouble, and will be followed by the Messiah's coming (Mt. 24:21, 29–31; 25:31–34). Daniel 11:40, then, refers to something that will take place during the future seven-year Tribulation.

The second question is this: Who is the "him" of verse 40 against whom the kings of the South and North will come militarily? Since the person described in Daniel 11:36–39 is the future Antichrist, it seems apparent that the "him" of verse 40 is also the Antichrist. Thus Daniel was being told that, in the future Tribulation, the Antichrist will be attacked jointly by the kings of the South and North.

That prompts the third question: Who are the king of the South and the king of the North in Daniel 11:40? Verses 1–35 of Daniel 11, which also refer to them, have already been fulfilled historically. In fact, they were fulfilled before the birth of Jesus Christ. Consequently, we know the king of the South in those verses was the ruler of Egypt, south of Israel; and the king of the North in those verses was the ruler of Syria, north of Israel. That is what they were in past history. Verse 40 has not yet been fulfilled.

Since Daniel was not told the kings of the South and North of verse 40 are to be different from those of verses 1–35, we are safe in concluding that the future king of the South is the ruler of Egypt and the future king of the North is the ruler of Syria. Thus Daniel was being told that in the future Tribulation, Egypt and Syria will jointly attack the Antichrist militarily.

But this revelation poses somewhat of a problem. On the one hand, Egypt and Syria are two nations in the Middle East. On the other hand, according to Daniel 7, the Antichrist will rule a future form of the Roman Empire. In addition, the end of Daniel 11:40 says, "and he shall enter the countries, overwhelm them, and pass through." Thus the Antichrist will invade the Middle East *as the result* of Egypt and Syria jointly attacking him. In other words, prior to their attack, he will be located somewhere other than the Middle East.

But if he will be located outside the Middle East before the attack, how will these two Middle Eastern nations attack him? Daniel 11 doesn't tell us, but Daniel 9:27 may shed light on the issue.

Daniel 9:27 reveals that the Antichrist will establish a seven-year covenant with the nation of Israel in the Middle East at the beginning of the seven-year Tribulation: "Then he shall confirm a covenant with many for one week." The word translated "week" literally means "seven" (God gave Israel a calendar system divided into seven-year periods, Lev. 25:1–5). Since Daniel 9:24 declares that all the years involved in this prophecy, including the seven years of verse 27, were determined by God specifically for Daniel's people Israel, it can be concluded that the "many" in Daniel 9:27 refers to the majority of the people in the nation of Israel. The word translated "confirm" means "to make a covenant strong."[2] It may indicate that the Antichrist will enforce this covenant on Israel.[3]

Apparently the Antichrist will want to have influence or a foothold in the Middle East. To accomplish that, this seven-year covenant will so strongly bind the nation of Israel to his Roman Empire that he will regard Israel as an extension of himself and his empire in the Middle East. As a result, he will consider any attack against Israel as an attack against himself and, therefore, will guarantee Israel's national security.

In light of Daniel 9:27, it appears the way Egypt and Syria will jointly attack the Antichrist during the future seven-year

Tribulation will be by jointly attacking his Middle East ally, Israel. Egypt will come up against Israel from the south, while Syria will come against it from the north in a pincer-type military attack.

How will the Antichrist react when he receives word of this attack against Israel? The end of Daniel 11:40 says, "and he shall enter the countries, overwhelm them, and pass through." Keeping his covenant commitment to Israel, he will invade the Middle East with his armed forces. The context of verse 40 implies that the Antichrist will invade north of Israel first in order to deal with Syria. Perhaps Lebanon will fall to him as well.

Then he will march his soldiers south through Israel ("He shall enter also into the Glorious Land," v. 41). But he won't take the time to cross over to the land east of the Jordan River where Edom, Moab, and Ammon were located in Old Testament times ("but these shall escape from his hand: Edom, Moab, and the prominent people of Ammon," v. 41). In other words, he won't take time to conquer the area occupied today by the nation of Jordan. He will purposely bypass that area in order to get to Egypt to deal with this other enemy of Israel.

Verse 42 indicates he will get to Egypt: "He shall stretch out his hand against the countries, and the land of Egypt shall not escape." Verse 43 states, "He shall have power over the treasures of gold and of silver, and over all the precious things of Egypt; also the Libyans and Ethiopians shall follow at his heels."

Two things should be noted concerning the expression "the Libyans and the Ethiopians shall follow at his heels." First, according to the *Wycliffe Bible Encyclopedia*, "The designation Ethiopia is misleading, for it did not refer to the modern state of Ethiopia or Abyssinia."[4] The word translated "Ethiopia" in verse 43 is "Cush." "The biblical Cush (Egyptian, *Kosh*) bordered Egypt on the S, the land of Nubia or modern Sudan."[5]

Second, the expression "at his heels" means that, when the Antichrist gets to Egypt's western border with Libya and southern border with Cush (modern Sudan), he will turn around so that these two countries will be at his heels. This indicates he will not invade these two nations, but he will conquer all of Egypt.

Verse 43 signifies that, once the Antichrist controls all of Egypt, he will begin to rob it of its resources and wealth. And it will look as if the Middle East were about to come under his domination.

However, while enjoying great success in Egypt, he will receive disturbing news from the east and north: "But news from the east and the north shall trouble him" (v. 44). The word translated "trouble" "usually expresses an emotion of one who is confronted with something unexpected, threatening or disastrous."[6] "More often it describes fear in battle."[7] This implies that the Antichrist will hear that an unexpected military force, so large that it threatens him and his ally Israel with disaster, has launched an invasion.

Israel vs. Iran, Sudan, Libya, Turkey, and Russia.
Ezekiel 38—39 reveals the military force and invasion that will threaten the Antichrist and his ally Israel while he is in Egypt. Ezekiel, a contemporary of Daniel, recorded divine revelation that, in the future, a massive military force from six nations (as they were known in Ezekiel and Daniel's time) will invade. Five of those nations are identified in Ezekiel 38:5–6. ·

The first nation, Persia, is now the modern state of Iran. Since the overthrow of the shah of Iran, that nation has been ruled by an Islamic fundamentalist government. In 1991 it hired Russian nuclear and missile scientists to help it develop nuclear warheads and missiles to deliver the warheads against enemies.[8] By 2006 it had obtained from North Korea long-range missiles capable of bombarding Europe.[9] Contrary to United Nations resolutions, Iran persists in developing its nuclear capability. Wrote Mort Zuckerman, "It has intensified its murderous anti-Semitic, anti-Israel rhetoric and reiterated its long-held position that the Middle East should be entirely Islamic, stripped of all western influence."[10] Iran's President Mahmoud Ahmadinejad has threatened to begin a nuclear holocaust that will annihilate Israel.

The second nation is listed as Ethiopia in the English Bible. But, as noted earlier in the exposition of Daniel 11:43, that is misleading. The word translated "Ethiopia" is "Cush" and refers to the land of Nubia, which today is not modern Ethiopia but Sudan, south of Egypt. Sudan is dominated by a brutal Arab Islamic fundamentalist government that murders, rapes, and enslaves Christians and animists and is slaughtering the black Muslims in Darfur in an attempt to establish a pure Islamic state.[11]

The third nation, Libya, Egypt's western neighbor, is also an Islamic nation. It is strongly anti-West and anti-Israel and supports terrorist activities. In the mid 1990s Western intelligence was informed that Libya had hired Eastern European and former Soviet military scientists to aid its development of military power.[12] Shortly after America and coalition forces attacked Iraq to bring down Saddam Hussein, Mu'ammar Qadhafi, the leader of Libya, announced that Libya would cease developing weapons of mass destruction. It remains to be seen if he kept his word. He is strongly anti-Israel.

The people of the fourth nation, Gomer, were also known as Cimmerians. They originally lived north of the Caucasus Mountains in the southern part of what is modern Russia. In Ezekiel's time they had settled in what is now central Turkey.[13]

The people of the fifth nation, Togarmah, were identified by Josephus as the Phrygians (*Antiquities* 1.6.1), who settled in Cappadocia, now eastern Turkey.[14]

Modern Turkey is an Islamic nation. Although it has had a secular government since 1923, it appears the Turkish people are becoming increasingly dissatisfied with it. As a result, fundamentalist Muslims are being elected to positions in various branches of the government. Because of certain trends in the 1990s, *U.S. News & World Report* published an article titled "Will Turkey be the next Iran?"[15] If Turkey comes under Islamic fundamentalist rule, it, too, will become an enemy of Israel.

The Leader of the Invasion. The five nations named in Ezekiel 38:5–6 will be led by a sixth nation in the future attack against Israel.

The leader's name is "Gog, of the land of Magog" (Ezek. 38:2). Jerome, a prominent church leader (A.D. 345–420), declared that Magog was located north of the Caucasus Mountains, near the Caspian Sea.[16] Josephus and Greek writers associated the name Magog with the Scythians.[17] According to the revised *International Standard Bible Encyclopedia*, the major group of Scythians lived near the Black Sea, "from the Caucasus around to the Danube."[18] It appears, then, that the land of Magog was located near the Black and Caspian Seas, north of the Caucasus Mountains, in the southern part of modern Russia.

The leader's political position is identified as "the prince of Rosh, Meshech, and Tubal" (vv. 2–3). Scholars disagree concerning the significance of the term *Rosh*. Some believe it was the name of a nation in Ezekiel's day from which the modern nation of Russia derived its name. But, although the Hebrew word *rosh* appears many other times in the Old Testament, "it never appears as a nation in any other biblical list of place names."[19] In addition, no ancient extrabiblical documents indicate that a nation with that name existed in Ezekiel's time, and the name Russia did not originate until the late 11th century A.D.[20]

Other scholars conclude *rosh* is a descriptive term referring to a position, not a proper name. The primary meaning of *rosh* is "head."[21] Thus it has the sense of "chief" or "ruler" in numerous Old Testament passages. One scholar observed that, in the Hebrew text of Ezekiel 38:2–3, *rosh* and the word translated "prince" are related grammatically "to the two geographical words Meshech and Tubal" in the same way.[22] This indicates that *rosh* is in apposition to "prince" and refers to the same ruling or leadership position as the word translated "prince." Thus the Hebrew grammar of Ezekiel 38:2–3 favors the following translation: "the prince, the chief ["head" or "ruler"] of Meshech and Tubal."[23] This is the position of rule that Gog will have as the leader of the future invasion of Israel.

Classical Greek writers called the people of Meshech the Moschoi, and Assyrian records referred to them as the Muski.[24]

This group settled in the area of Armenia, "where the borders of Russia, Iran and Turkey converge."[25]

The people of Tubal were located in the central part of Turkey immediately west of Togarmah.[26]

The leader's geographical location is described as "the far north." God said to Gog, "you will come from your place out of the far north" (Ezek. 38:15; 39:2). The Hebrew word translated "far" means "extreme or uttermost parts."[27] Since the target of Gog's attack will be Israel, it is obvious that he will be coming from his location in the extreme or uttermost parts directly north of Israel. Russia is clearly the nation directly north of Israel. There is no other nation farther north of Israel than Russia.

Why would Russia lead the future invasion against Israel, foretold in Ezekiel 38—39? One reason is anti-Semitism. Before Communism, Russia was notorious for brutally persecuting the Jewish people. This prompted a mass migration of Jews to Western Europe and the Americas in the late 19th and early 20th centuries. As long as Communism held the Russian government in its iron grip, it suppressed the outward expression of hatred for the Jews. When Communism lost its grip in the early 1990s with the fracturing of the Soviet Union, anti-Semitism reared its ugly head again. This prompted another Jewish exodus, with the majority returning to its ancient homeland of Israel.

A second reason for Russia to lead the future invasion of Israel is a desire for status. With the removal of the Berlin Wall, the freeing of Central and Eastern European nations from Soviet domination, and the fracturing of the Soviet Union during the last segment of the 20th century, Russia lost its superpower status of the Cold War era. Some of Russia's early 21st-century policies seem to indicate it is seeking to regain superpower status by allying itself with Islamic nations that are determined to eliminate Israel.

During the Cold War, part of Russia's status involved working with Islamic nations to block American influence in the Middle East. For example, it supplied Syria and Egypt with military weapons to use in their wars against America's Middle East ally, Israel.

One indication that Russia continues that approach in the 21st century is its supply of weapons to Hezbollah in Lebanon and Hamas in Gaza to use in their wars against Israel. It is common knowledge that those weapons were delivered from Russia via Syria and Iran.

Another indication of this approach is Russia's policies with Iran. Shiite Iran is developing into the regional superpower of the Middle East.[28] It greatly influences what happens in southern Iraq, Syria, Lebanon, the West Bank, and Gaza; and it poses an increasing threat to the Sunni Arab nations of Saudi Arabia, Egypt, Kuwait, and the United Arab Emirates.[29] It is also sending combatants into Afghanistan and "supporting terrorists against Turkey."[30] Iran's President Mahmoud Ahmadinejad has stated, "We are in the process of an historical war between the World of Arrogance [i.e., the West] and the Islamic world."[31]

Perhaps it is because Russia also opposes the influence of the West, especially that of America, that it has been aiding Iran's development into a regional superpower. Wrote Zuckerman: "It sold the nuclear power plant at Bushehr to Iran and contracted to sell even more to bring cash into its nuclear industry."[32] It also "provided critical assistance in the development of Iran's Shihab missile, which has an ever expanding delivery range and can carry a warhead designed for a nuclear charge."[33] Russian President Vladimir Putin supported Iran's resistance of the International Atomic Energy Agency's attempts to keep Iran's developing nuclear program under close scrutiny.[34] Russia has resisted UN Security Council attempts to impose stringent economic sanctions on Iran if it persists in developing nuclear weapons. In addition, it has assisted Iran in developing an effective system of defense against enemy attack by selling it "TOR-M1 surface-to-air missiles, the most advanced system available, which uses launchers to shoot down multiple targets like missiles and planes."[35]

These Russian policies toward Islamic nations seem to imply that Russia believes it can regain superpower status in the world if it will ally itself with Islamic nations in opposition to the West and Israel.

However, there is a third possible reason for Russia to lead the future invasion of Israel. Present trends indicate that, unless things change in the near future, Russia will become an Islamic majority state within several decades. Russian people are not propagating enough children to maintain the Russian population in their native country. Many younger Russian women refuse to have children. The majority of those who do, limit themselves to one child.[36] A high Russian abortion rate contributes to this trend. Demographers who study population growth predict that, if this trend continues, the Russian population will decline from 143 million to 100 million by 2050.[37]

By contrast, almost all Muslim couples in Russia have three to five children.[38] Consequently, in Russia "the Muslim population growth rate since 1989 is between 40 and 50 percent."[39] In 1991 there were 300 mosques in Russia. In 2006 there were approximately 8,000. It is estimated that by the end of 2015, Russia will have about 25, 000 mosques.[40]

Another trend is the large number of Islamist religious clerics who are winning Russian converts from other religions and atheism to Islam.[41] Afro-Arab Muslims are pouring millions of dollars into this missionary endeavor.[42]

In light of these trends, the "number of Muslim journalists is increasing steadily," and a considerable "number of important seats in the Russian parliament will also go into the hands of Muslim leaders."[43] Muslim clerics operate orphanages in Russia as a means of converting children to Islam.[44]

If Russia becomes an Islamic nation, it will join other Islamic nations in the desire to eliminate Israel.

The Time of the Invasion. In Ezekiel 38:8, 16, God declared that this future invasion of Israel will take place "in the latter years" and "latter days." As we noted earlier, Jews in biblical times divided all of history since the fall of man into two ages: before Messiah comes to rule the world (to their way of thinking, that is the present age) and when Messiah is present ruling the world ("the age to come" or "the Messianic age").

The Scriptures reveal that no military warfare will take place during Messiah's reign in the future Messianic age (Isa. 2:1–4; 9:6–7). By contrast, Ezekiel 38:8–16 indicates that military warfare will take place "in the latter years" and "latter days." So the invasion of Israel by Gog and his allies will take place "in the latter years" and "latter days" of the present age, before Messiah comes to rule the world in the future Kingdom of God. It cannot take place during the future Millennium.

Since other prophetic passages reveal that the end-times of the present age will be characterized by tribulation, including an unparalleled time of trouble (Mt. 24:21, 29–31; 25:31–34), we must conclude that the Ezekiel 38 invasion of Israel will take place during the future seven-year Tribulation.

Ezekiel 38:8, 11–12, 14 indicate it will happen after Israel has been regathered to its homeland and feels so safe and secure that it has no defenses of its own. There has been an amazing regathering of Israel to its homeland since its reestablishment there as a nation-state in 1948. But because of repeated attacks against it and the continuing desire of its enemies to eliminate it, Israel has never had the luxury of feeling so safe and secure as to have no need for defenses of its own. It has, in fact, been forced to maintain its defenses with some of the most advanced military hardware and highly trained armed forces in the history of mankind.

Will there be a time before Messiah's coming to rule the world in the future political Kingdom of God when Israel will feel so safe and secure that it will not maintain its defenses? It appears so. Daniel 9:27 reveals that, at the outset of the future seven-year Tribulation, the Antichrist will establish a covenant with Israel that will so strongly bind Israel to him that he will regard the nation as an extension of himself and his empire and will guarantee Israel's national security. This covenant will cause Israel to feel so safe and secure that it will discontinue the costly burden of maintaining its own defenses.

This feeling of security will not last long, however. Daniel 9:27 indicates that, in the middle of the seven-year period, the Antichrist will begin to desolate Israel (cf. Mt. 24:15–21). Thus the nation will feel safe and secure only during the first half of the Tribulation. In light of this fact and the revelation of Ezekiel 38:8, 11–12, 14 that the invasion of Israel will take place while it feels safe and secure, it can be concluded that the invasion of Israel by Russia and its allies will take place during the first half of the Tribulation, probably shortly before its midpoint.

The Invaders' Attitude and Actions. Gog and his allies will think that, since Israel has let down its guard militarily, their opportune time has come to strike Israel and plunder its resources (Ezek. 38:10–13). As a result, they will launch such a massive invasion that the forces will look like an enormous cloud covering the land (vv. 9, 15–16).

Because of its location east of Israel, Iran will invade from the east. Since Russia and Turkey are situated north of Israel, they will attack from the north. Since Sudan and Libya are located south and west of Israel, under normal circumstances they would move their forces through Egypt in order to invade Israel from the south. But, in light of Daniel 11:42–43, Israel's ally, the Antichrist, will control Egypt. So instead of going through Egypt, Sudan and Libya will need to move their forces across the Mediterranean Sea in order to join the forces of Russia and Turkey north of Israel. Thus this alignment has Iran attacking Israel from the east and Russia, Turkey, Sudan, and Libya invading Israel from the north. It fits the scenario of Daniel 11:43–44 that reveals that, while the Antichrist is in control of Egypt, he will receive news from the east and the north that will trouble him.

God's Attitude and Actions. God's initial action will be to pull Russia and its allies into Israel for His own sovereign purpose. He declared,

Behold, I am against you, O Gog, the prince of Rosh, Meshech, and Tubal. I will turn you around, put hooks into your jaws, and lead you out, with all your army, horses, and horsemen, all splendidly clothed, a great company with bucklers and shields, all of them handling swords. Persia, Ethiopia, and Libya are with them, all of them with shield and helmet; Gomer and all its troops; the house of Togarmah from the far north and all its troops—many people are with you. You will come up against My people Israel like a cloud, to cover the land. It will be in the latter days that I will bring you against My land, so that the nations may know Me, when I am hallowed in you, O Gog, before their eyes. I will turn you around and lead you on, bringing you up from the far north, and bring you against the mountains of Israel (Ezek. 38:3–6, 16; 39:2).

When they invade Israel, God's attitude toward them will be characterized by fury, jealousy, and fiery wrath: "'And it will come to pass at the same time, when Gog comes against the land of Israel,' says the Lord GOD, 'that My fury will show in My face. For in My jealousy and in the fire of My wrath I have spoken'" (38:18–19).

The word translated "fury" refers to God's "hot displeasure."[45] The word translated "jealousy" indicates "zeal for one's own property."[46] In Ezekiel 38, verses 14 and 16, God refers to "MY people Israel" and "MY land" (emphasis added). He thereby signifies that the people of Israel and the land of Israel are owned exclusively by Him. Thus, when Russia and its allies invade Israel, He will react with intense zeal to protect His property.

The word translated "wrath" emphasizes "the fierceness of God's wrath expressed in an overwhelming and complete demonstration. God's wrath burns, overflows, sweeps away everything before it."[47]

In His fury, jealousy, and fiery wrath, God will intervene directly and supernaturally into world events to destroy the massive invading forces of Russia and its allies in the land of Israel. He will cause a fierce earthquake, landslides, the collapse of walls, a self-destructive panic, and pestilence, to bombard the invaders. He also will bring excessive rain, great hailstones, fire, and brimstone on them (vv. 19–22).

The destruction of the invaders will be so extensive that the mountains and open fields of Israel and a valley near the Dead Sea will be congested with corpses. God will bring fowl and beasts to devour many of them. It will take the Jewish people seven months to bury the remainder of the dead and seven years to destroy their weapons (39:3–5, 9–20). If this invasion takes place shortly before the middle of the Tribulation, the destruction of these weapons will continue into the early part of the future Millennium, when Messiah rules the world.

God's purpose for all of this will be to glorify Himself before Israel and all the nations—to so impress them with His existence and power that He will have life-changing influence on them (38:16, 23; 39:7, 13, 21–22). Many Jewish and Gentile people will be saved during the future Tribulation (Rev. 7). No doubt the fulfillment of the Ezekiel 38—39 prophecy will be one of the means through which God will bring people of that time to Himself.

The Activity of the Antichrist. The latter half of Daniel 11:44 reveals how the Antichrist will react to the news from the east and the north that will trouble him while he is in Egypt: "Therefore he shall go out with great fury to destroy and annihilate many." Keeping his covenant commitment to his ally Israel, he will rush his armed forces north from Egypt with the goal of destroying the forces of Russia and its allies. However, when he arrives in Israel he will discover that those forces have been destroyed totally apart from any human activity.

That destruction will give him a free hand to do whatever he desires in the Middle East. As a result, he will set up his headquarters in Jerusalem (at "the glorious holy mountain"—either Mount Zion or the Temple Mount, where Israel's capital city is located, between the Dead and Mediterranean Seas; Dan. 11:45).

At this point, the world will have arrived at the middle of the seven-year Tribulation. Daniel 9:27 reveals that, once the Antichrist is free to do what he wants in the Middle East and has control of Jerusalem, "He shall bring an end to sacrifice and offering" "in the middle" of that seven-year period. In other words, in the middle of those seven years, He will take control of Israel's next Temple and end the Old Testament order of priesthood and sacrifices that the Jews will have reestablished by that time. He will do this so that he can take his seat there and make the blasphemous claim that he is God:

> *Then the king shall do according to his own will: he shall exalt and magnify himself above every god, shall speak blasphemies against the God of gods, and shall prosper till the wrath has been accomplished; for what has been determined shall be done. He shall regard neither the God of his fathers nor the desire of women, nor regard any god; for he shall exalt himself above them all* (Dan. 11:36–37).

Scripture says, "the man of sin is revealed, the son of perdition, who opposes and exalts himself above all that is called God or that is worshiped, so that he sits as God in the temple of God, showing himself that he is God" (2 Th. 2:3–4). It may be that the Antichrist will claim credit for the supernatural destruction of the forces of Russia and its allies as support for his assertion that he is God.

Immediately after Daniel 11:45, the next verse (12:1) reveals that, when the Antichrist will take control of Jerusalem and the Temple and claim to be God, the unparalleled time of trouble in all of history will begin: "At that time Michael shall stand up, the great prince who stands watch over the sons of your people; and there shall be a time of trouble, such as never was since there was a nation, even to that time." In Daniel 12:6 an angel asked how long this unparalleled time of trouble would last. The answer was, "for a time, times, and half a time" (v. 7). In Daniel that expression always refers to three and one-half years. This indicates that the Antichrist's activity of taking control of Jerusalem and the Temple and claiming to be God will take place in the middle of the seven-year Tribulation and begin its second half.

Revelation 13:4–6 indicates that, once the Antichrist makes the blasphemous claim to be God and begins to be worshiped, he will be given power to continue for 42 months. Forty-two months equal three and one-half years. This again signifies that it is that activity that will take place in the middle of the seven-year Tribulation and begin its second half.

Conclusion

Daniel 11:40–45 and Ezekiel 38—39 teach that the nation of Israel will have serious problems with Egypt, Syria, Iran, Sudan, Libya, Turkey, and Russia in the future. All of these nations except Russia entered the 21st century overwhelmingly Islamic in their worldview, and Russia could become Islamic within several decades. If these nations continue to be Islamic to the time that the prophecies of Daniel 11:40–45 and Ezekiel 38—39 are fulfilled, then (1) Israel will continue to have serious problems with Islamic nations into the extended future and (2) these Islamic nations will suffer severe judgment from God.

It is important to understand why God will judge these Islamic nations. He will judge them because of their attempt to annihilate the nation of Israel in the Middle East. For His own sovereign purposes, God chose Israel for a unique relationship with Him, and He intends it to play a key role in the fulfillment of His plan and purpose for mankind and history. Therefore, He jealously watches over that nation and will faithfully prevent it from being eliminated.

God will not judge these Islamic nations because He hates their people in contrast with the people of other nations. God has demonstrated His love as fully for Muslims as for all others. He sent His Son, Jesus Christ, to die for the sins of all mankind and be resurrected from the dead. He did this so that all people who place their trust in Jesus Christ to be their personal Savior can have full forgiveness of their sins and God's gift of eternal life.

Consequently, Christians should demonstrate God's love for

Muslims by warning them that God always judges those who try to annihilate the nation of Israel and Jewish people and by presenting to them the Good News of eternal salvation that God has lovingly provided for them through the sacrifice and resurrection of His Son.

ENDNOTES

[1] Hermann Sasse, "aion," *Theological Dictionary of the New Testament* (hereafter cited as *TDNT*), ed. Gerhard Kittel, ed./trans. Geoffrey W. Bromiley, translated from *Theologisches Worterbuch zum Neuen Testament* (Grand Rapids: Eerdmans, 1964), 1:206–207. Also, William F. Arndt and F. Wilbur Gingrich, eds./trans., "aion," *A Greek English Lexicon of the New Testament and Other Early Christian Literature* (1952: translation and adaptation of Walter Bauer's *Griechisch-Deutsches Worterbuch zu den Schriften des Neuen Testaments und der ubrigen urchristlichen Literatur,* 4th ed.; Chicago: University of Chicago Press, 1957), 27. Also, Raphael Patai, *The Messiah Texts* (Detroit: Wayne State University Press, 1979), XIII, XVII.

[2] C. F. Keil, *Biblical Commentary on the Book of Daniel* (Grand Rapids: Eerdmans, 1959), 366.

[3] Ibid.

[4] Philip C. Johnson, "Cush," *Wycliffe Bible Encyclopedia,* ed. Charles F. Pfeiffer, Howard F. Vos, and John Rea (Chicago: Moody Press, 1975), 1:411.

[5] Ibid.

[6] Elmer A. Martens, " bahal," *Theological Wordbook of the Old Testament* (hereafter cited as *TWOT*), ed. Laird Harris, Gleason L. Archer Jr., and Bruce K. Waltke (Chicago: Moody Press, 1980), 1:92.

[7] Benedikt Otzen, "bahal," *Theological Dictionary of the Old Testament,* ed. Johannes Botterweck and Helmer Ringgren, trans. John T. Willis, translated from *Theologisches Worterbuch zum Alten Testament* (Grand Rapids: Eerdmans, 1977), 2:4.

[8] C. Fenyvesi, "Brain Drain," *U.S. News & World Report* 111, no. 20 (Nov. 11, 1991): 30.

[9] Mortimer B. Zuckerman, "The Mullah Menace," *U.S. News & World Report* 141, no. 22 (December 11, 2006): 88.

[10] Ibid.

[11] Elwood McQuaid, "A Window in Sudan," *Israel My Glory* 52 (April/May 1994): 4–5.

[12] Fenyvesi.

[13] J. J. Reeve and Roland K. Harrison, "Gomer," *International Standard Bible Encyclopedia,* rev. ed. ed. Geoffrey Bromiley (Grand Rapids: Eerdmans, 1982), 2:524.

[14] C. J. Hemer, "Togarmah," *International Standard Bible Encyclopedia,* rev. ed. (1988), 4:868. Hemer, "Cappadocia" (1979), 1:611.

[15] Fred Coleman, "Will Turkey be the next Iran?" *U.S. News & World Report* 116, no. 22 (June 6, 1994): 51.

[16] "Gog and Magog," *The Jewish Encyclopedia* (New York: Funk and Wagnalls, 1904), 6:19.

[17] Clyde E. Harrington, *The New International Dictionary of the Bible* (Grand Rapids: Zondervan, 1987), 614.

[18] A. R. Millard, "Scythians," *International Standard Bible Encyclopedia*, 4:365.

[19] Charles H. Dyer, "Ezekiel," *The Bible Knowledge Commentary*, ed. John F. Walvoord and Roy B. Zuck (Wheaton, ILL: Victor Books, 1985), 1:1299.

[20] Ralph H. Alexander, "Ezekiel," *The Expositor's Bible Commentary*, ed. Frank E. Gaebelein (Grand Rapids: Zondervan, 1986), 6:930.

[21] William White, " rosh," *TWOT*, 2:825.

[22] Alexander, "Ezekiel."

[23] Ibid.

[24] J. A. Lees, "Meshech," *International Standard Bible Encyclopedia*, rev. ed. (1986), 3:328.

[25] W. W. Gasque, "Ararat," *International Standard Bible Encyclopedia* (1979), 1:233.

[26] P. K. McCarter, Jr., "Tubal," *International Standard Bible Encyclopedia* (1988), 4:928.

[27] John E. Hartley, "yarka," *TWOT*, 1:408.

[28] Zuckerman, "The Mullah Menace," 88.

[29] Ibid.

[30] Mortimer B. Zuckerman, "Moscow's Mad Gamble," *U.S. News & World Report* 140, no. 4 (January 30/February 6, 2006): 76.

[31] Ibid., cited by Mortimer B. Zuckerman.

[32] Ibid.

[33] ibid.

[34] Ibid.

[35] Ibid.

[36] Salah Uddin Shoaib Choudhury, "Russia becoming a Muslim state!" *Asian Tribune*, May 22, 2006 <asiantribune.com/index.php?q=node/211>.

[37] Ibid.

[38] Ibid.

[39] Ibid.

[40] Ibid.

[41] Ibid.

[42] Ibid.

[43] Ibid.

[44] Ibid.

[45] Gerard Van Groningen, "hema," *TWOT*, 1:374.

[46] Leonard J. Coppes, "qana," *TWOT*, 2:802.

[47] Gerard Van Groningen, "ebra," *TWOT*, 2:643.

EDITOR'S POSTSCRIPT

Many years ago one of our Friends of Israel workers preached a message on the end-times in a solid, Bible-believing church. In discussing Zechariah 12, where God promises to deliver Israel from all the nations that will try to destroy it, he declared, "Someday the entire world will turn against Israel."

When he finished, an irate woman accosted him as he greeted people at the door and chided him fiercely for implying the United States would turn its back on the Jewish nation. He replied, "I love Israel as much as you do, ma'am. But if the United States is still around then, it will turn on Israel, too, because God said, 'I will gather all the nations to battle against Jerusalem'" (Zech. 14:2).

Today, as anti-Semitism grows exponentially and the political winds shift in favor of Islam and the Palestinians, it is not difficult to see the truth of God's end-times prophecies. Little Israel is becoming despised and isolated in a world now characterized by vicious hostility toward the God of the Bible. The closer we get to the Rapture, when God will remove all true Christians from the earth prior to the Time of Jacob's Trouble (Tribulation), the closer America and the West move to abandoning all support for Israel.

Israel's situation has grown so precarious, in fact, that it even came to the fore in the November 2008 attack in Mumbai, India, where the Jewish community is extremely small. When Islamic terrorists infiltrated the country and massacred about 200 people in the city's luxury hotels, they also targeted the modest, unassuming, ultra-Orthodox Chabad Lubavitch House run by a 28-year-old rabbi. They savagely murdered Rabbi Gavriel Holtzberg and his pregnant wife, Rivka. A doctor who performed the postmortem said, "Of all the bodies, the Israeli victims bore the maximum torture marks. It was obvious that they were tied up and tortured before they were killed. It was so bad that I do not want to go over the details even in my head again."

Israel National News, which reported the doctor's comments, also reported that the lone surviving murderer "told officials that the terrorists 'were specifically asked to target the foreigners, especially the Israelis.'" After the massacre, a television news commentator observed that Israel is becoming such an overt object of international terrorism that if someone does not rise up soon to help the tiny nation, it may not survive.

From a human perspective, the commentator appears correct. But Israel will survive because of the faithfulness of Almighty God, who loves His Chosen People and will rescue them Himself:

> *Then the LORD will go forth and fight against those nations, as He fights in the day of battle. And in that day His feet will stand on the Mount of Olives which faces Jerusalem on the east. And the Mount of Olives shall be split in two. And this shall be the plague with which the LORD will strike all the people who fought against Jerusalem: Their flesh shall dissolve while they stand on their feet, their eyes shall dissolve in their sockets, and their tongues shall dissolve in their mouths. It shall come to pass in that day that a great panic from the LORD will be among them* (Zech. 14:3–4, 12–13).

God will most assuredly deliver Israel. No other nation on Earth has received this guarantee: "'For I am with you,' says the LORD 'to save you; though I make a full end of all nations where I have scattered you, yet I will not make a complete end of you'" (Jer. 30:11).

In the meantime, the Jewish nation has a long, difficult journey ahead of it. And unfortunately, Christians who should know better and who should believe that when God makes a promise, He keeps it, are being sucked into the vortex of Replacement Theology, which is siphoning off support for Israel. As the fight over the land and the city of Jerusalem intensifies, fewer Christians will stand with Israel; and their defection makes the truth of the prophetic Scriptures even more obvious.

In the coming apocalypse, two-thirds of Earth's inhabitants will die, including two-thirds of the Jewish people. But at the end of the seven-year Tribulation (also called Daniel's 70th Week), Christ will return. He will rescue Israel from the world's armies and the clutches of the Antichrist, and He will set everything right.

Perhaps no prophecy in Scripture better describes the Tribulation's purpose than Daniel 9:24. When the angel Gabriel came to the Jewish prophet Daniel in the 6th century B.C., he explained that God will use the Time of Jacob's Trouble "to finish the transgression, to make an end of sins, to make reconciliation for iniquity, to bring in everlasting righteousness, to seal up vision and prophecy, and to anoint the Most Holy." None of these events has yet come to pass. Humanity, for the most part, still rejects God; sin runs rampant; *everlasting* righteousness has not arrived on planet Earth; unfulfilled prophecy still exists; and the Messiah has not been anointed King or taken His seat on David's throne. All these things are yet future.

The good news is that Israel not only will survive what lies ahead but will come through the fire; be reconciled to its Messiah; and enjoy safety, prosperity, and peace in the land God promised to give to the physical descendants of Abraham, Isaac, and Jacob. And because God is faithful to Israel, we can trust Him to be faithful to His church as well.

GENERAL INDEX

SCRIPTURE INDEX